U. S. ARMY RESEARCH LABORATORY

MISSION: Discover, innovate, and transition science and technology to ensure dominant strategic land power.

VISION: The nation's premier laboratory for land forces.

U. S. Army Research Laboratory S&T Campaign Plans

Table of Contents

INTRODUCTION

The U.S. Army Research Laboratory (ARL) is the Department of the Army's corporate laboratory, strategically placed within the Army Materiel Command (AMC), an *institutional* Army Command (ACOM). ARL is also the Army's sole fundamental research laboratory focused on scientific discovery, technological innovation, and transition of knowledge products; it impacts the Army and broader DoD science and technology (S&T) communities through transition of knowledge products to its sister Research, Development, and Engineering Centers (RDECs) within the Army Research, Development, and Engineering Command (RDECOM) – an AMC Major Subordinate Command (MSC), Army PMs/PEOs, the other services, and industry. ARL executes fundamental research, defined as Basic Research (BA 1) and Applied Research (BA 2), to address enduring S&T challenges that have been identified by the Assistant Secretary of the Army for Acquisition, Logistics, and Technology [ASA(ALT)] and priorities articulated by the Chief of Staff of the Army (CSA). In addition, the laboratory conducts research in emerging fields that hold promise in realization of novel or vastly improved Army capabilities into the deep future; performs research on behalf of other Army activities and, where specifically qualified, for other agencies of the DoD; and, in defense-related efforts, for other government agencies (OGAs). Explicitly, ARL's mission is to *"Discover, innovate, and transition science and technology to ensure dominant strategic land power"*; to achieve these goals, the laboratory maintains a broad-based, multidisciplinary technical portfolio dedicated to fundamental research to support the Army's strategic land power dominance through new and greatly improved methodologies, techniques, and materials.

Founded on the tenets of discovery, innovation, and transition, ARL drives opportunities in power projection, information, lethality & protection, and Soldier performance for the Army of 2030 and beyond using a framework of eight S&T Campaigns – *a systematic course of aggressive science and technology activities envisioned to lead to enhanced land power capabilities in the deep future*. These S&T Campaigns – in Extramural Basic Research; Computational Sciences; Materials Research; Sciences-for-Maneuver; Information Sciences; Sciences-for-Lethality & Protection; Human Sciences; and Assessment & Analysis – operate in concert to provide ARL with a robust technological foundation to execute its mission. More, each of these S&T Campaigns is designed to explore, better understand, mature, and exploit S&T developments leading to Power Projection Superiority, Information Supremacy, Lethality & Protection Superiority, and Soldier Performance Augmentation that are essential to the future Army.

This document defines each of ARL's S&T Campaign Plans and is an appendix to the Army Research Laboratory Technical Strategy (April 2014). It is intended to provide additional insight into the technical areas that ARL believes are critical to the Army's assured land power dominance into the deep future. Each S&T Campaign Plan provides a high-level overview of the campaign's technical landscape; a taxonomic breakdown of the campaign; descriptions of the technical areas constituting the campaign; and defines ARL's S&T Footprint in these areas including the laboratory's posture relative to the S&T area – whether we will LEAD, COLLABORATE, or WATCH.

LEAD is defined as a posture in which ARL maintains considerable in-house expertise, substantive infrastructure, and devotes significant investment based on unique Army needs. ARL leads in areas when it is imperative and when only we will or can.

COLLABORATE is defined as a posture in which ARL establishes an interdependent partnership with another Army S&T organization, DoD S&T agency, other government agency (OGA), academic institution, or industrial interest to pursue Army-relevant research goals. Through these partnerships, ARL provides its research partner with access to unique infrastructure, technological advances, and in-house expertise that significantly influence the research direction of the collaboration. Collaborating allows ARL's in-house technical experts to exploit technologies that they may not have otherwise been afforded the opportunity to develop.

WATCH is defined as a posture in which ARL maintains high vigilance in monitoring emerging technologies and corresponding R&D efforts within industry, academia, and international markets. ARL accomplishes this through active engagement in the national and international scientific dialog to remain poised to react to developments that make the area a viable approach towards Army capability challenges. Technology areas that are typically watched include those without unique Army requirements and where the Army can allow technology development to proceed with limited Army S&T involvement.

Each of ARL's S&T Campaigns is described by a taxonomy containing up to five levels; where Level 1 is the S&T Campaign title. The taxonomic syntax for levels 2 through 5 in each campaign plan is as follows.

LEVEL 2 – Level 2 taxonomy items are represented by capitalized bold script.

Level 3 – Level 3 taxonomy items are represented by bold script.

Level 4 – Level 4 taxonomy items (where applicable) are represented by italicized bold script.

(i) Level 5 – Level 5 taxonomy items (where applicable) are enumerated with Roman numerals and represented by italicized script.

EXTRAMURAL BASIC RESEARCH CAMPAIGN

MISSION: To steer and oversee Army-relevant technical programs executed by ARL's academic and corporate partners in the engineering, physical, information and life sciences; and develop and exploit innovative advances to ensure the Nation's technological superiority. Discoveries and innovations generated through these programs – primarily embodied as knowledge products – are leveraged as the foundation for future Army technologies.

VISION: Discoveries and innovations made with our academic and industrial partners are infused into the Army's S&T laboratory portfolio to provide a robust foundation for technical advances ensuring the Army's technological edge. High relevance discoveries and innovations are strongly leveraged by the Army's S&T laboratory enterprise to achieve capabilities far beyond the state-of-the-art. Discoveries and innovations made through collaborative efforts are essential in maintaining the land power dominance of the Army of 2030 and beyond.

EXTRAMURAL BASIC RESEARCH CAMPAIGN PLAN

ARL's Extramural Basic Research Campaign is focused on identifying, forming, driving, and transitioning innovative research discoveries in the Physical Sciences, Information Sciences, Life Sciences, and Engineering Sciences that are critical to the U.S. Army's future technological superiority. This campaign concentrates on high-risk and high-payoff transformational basic research that is expected to have revolutionary impacts on the Army's warfighting capabilities. In addition to significantly improving the Army's existing warfighting capabilities, it creates disruptive and game-changing new technologies for the Army, while also preventing technological surprises from potential adversaries.

The Extramural Basic Research Campaign provides critical underpinning support to all of the other ARL Campaigns, feeding new ideas and concepts into those campaigns, and also providing key connections with world-class extramural researchers to perform collaborative research with ARL's scientists and engineers. Additionally, when unique and important opportunities exist, research is also supported with industry partners, not-for profit organizations, other research organizations, and international researchers.

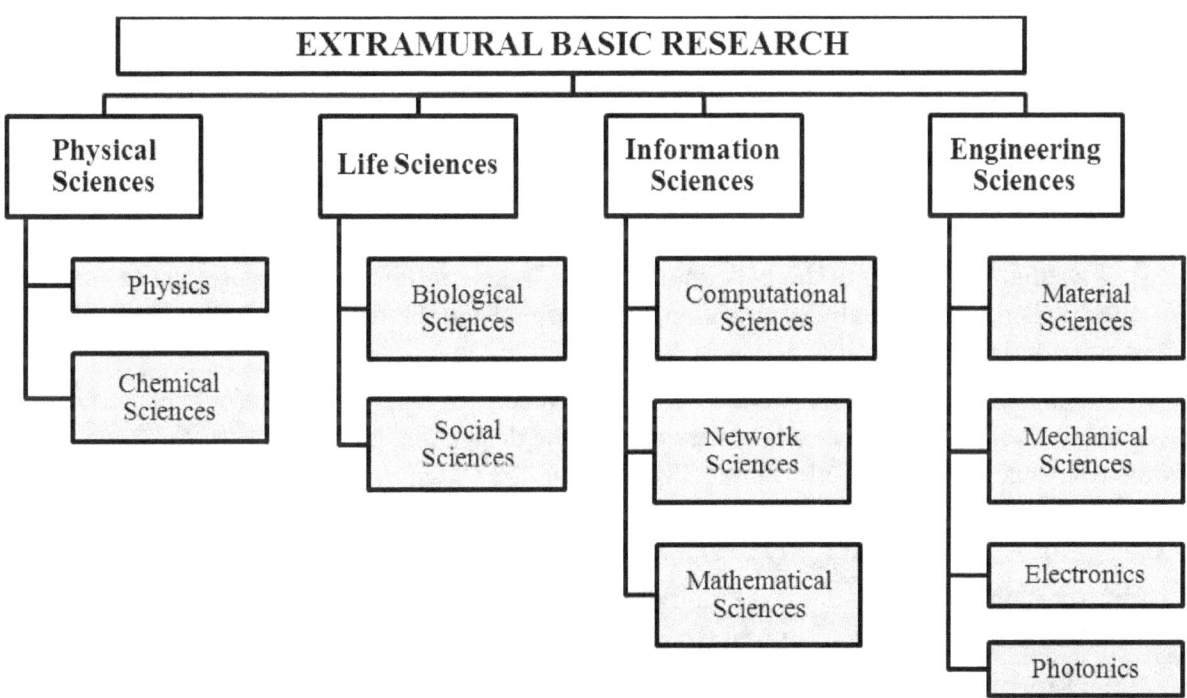

Levels 1 through 3 of the Extramural Basic Research Campaign Plan Taxonomy

PHYSICAL SCIENCES is focused on basic research to discover, understand, and exploit physical phenomena which are expected to create revolutionary capabilities for the Army of 2030 and beyond. Discoveries in this area are expected to lead to capabilities in communications and materials well beyond classical limits that restrict the performance of current Army systems.

Physics performs research to discover and understand exotic quantum and extreme optical physics where new regimes are expected to create revolutionary capabilities for the future warfighter.

Atomic and Molecular Physics pursues greater understanding of quantum properties of atoms, molecules, and exotic quantum behavior, including matter wave interference, lasing, diffraction, and up/down-conversion. The long-term applications of this research are broad and include ultra-sensitive detectors, precision time and frequency, novel sources, atom lasers and atom holography, and design of strongly correlated materials from first principles.

(i) State-dependant Quantum Chemistry is focused on the underlying mechanisms of molecules and reactions, such as electronic transport, magnetic response, coherence properties, and/or linear and nonlinear optical properties.

(ii) Topological Quantum Matter is focused exploiting the dimensionality and engineered interactions of quantum systems to provide novel global properties, for improved robustness, novel sensing, and computation. Topological quantum systems form persistent quasi-particles separated spatially, making them robust to local perturbations such as scattering and heating. These systems provide longer experimental interaction times and unique symmetry capabilities to provide new scientific opportunities. The Extramural Basic Research Campaign collaborates with AFOSR to coordinate complementary efforts and strategy in this area.

(iii) Precision Navigation Using Atom Interferometry explores the use of cold atom systems for improved sensing applications, particularly for GPS-independent navigation. The Extramural Basic Research Campaign is collaborating with and following AFRL-led research in this area.

Condensed Matter Physics is focused on discovery and characterization of novel quantum phases of matter at oxide-oxide interfaces and at surfaces and interfaces of topological insulators. Recent studies have shown that interfaces can support quantum phases that are foreign to the bulk constituents. In general the interface provides a mechanism for potentially controlling lattice, orbital, spin and charge structure in ways not possible in bulk, single-phase materials.

(i) Complex Oxide Heterostructures is focused on discovering new electronic phases of matter resulting from strong correlations, and the design and control of quantum many-body phenomena. The Extramural Basic Research Campaign collaborates with ONR, AFOSR, and DARPA through complementary research efforts.

(ii) Topologically-protected Electronic States seeks to achieve surface-dominated transport phenomena and to explore many-body effects in topologically-protected electronic states. The Extramural Basic Research Campaign collaborates with ONR, AFOSR, and DARPA in complementary research in topological insulators.

(iii) Superconductivity is exploring new materials that could extend superconductivity to higher temperatures, ideally to the room temperature regime. The Extramural Basic Research Campaign is following AFOSR's extensive program in this research area.

Quantum Information Science focuses on creation and control of nonclassical states for revolutionary capabilities in computation, sensing, and secure communications.

(i) Quantum Encoding explores the wave nature of matter, including coherence properties, decoherence mechanisms, decoherence mitigation, entanglement, nondestructive measurement, complex quantum state manipulation, and quantum feedback. The objective is to ascertain current limits in creating, controlling, and utilizing information encoded in quantum systems in the presence of noise.

(ii) Quantum Computation and Communication entails experimental demonstrations of quantum logic with multiple quantum bits operating simultaneously including demonstrations of quantum feedback and error correction. Quantum communication involves studies of the transmission of information through quantum entanglement, distributed between spatially separated quantum entities. Long-range entanglement transfer among different quantum systems and long-term quantum memory are of interest. The Extramural Basic Research Campaign leads research in this area, while also collaborating with AFOSR in the subfield of hybrid quantum systems and quantum memory.

(iii) Quantum Sensing and Metrology is an emerging field of interest. Quantum entanglement provides a means of exceeding classical limits in sensing and metrology and the goal is to demonstrate this experimentally.

(iv) Quantum Key Distribution explores a range of quantum-based methods for ultra-secure communications. The Extramural Basic Research Campaign follows the significant ONR and DARPA investments in this area.

EXTRAMURAL BASIC RESEARCH CAMPAIGN's Physics S&T Footprint	
S&T AREA	**POSTURE**
State-dependant Quantum Chemistry	LEAD
Topological Quantum Matter	COLLABORATE
Precision Navigation Using Atom Interferometry	WATCH
Complex Oxide Heterostructures	WATCH
Topologically-protected Electronic States	COLLABORATE
Superconductivity	WATCH
Quantum Encoding	LEAD
Quantum Computation and Communication	COLLABORATE
Quantum Sensing and Metrology	LEAD
Quantum Key Distribution	WATCH

Chemical Sciences performs research to discover and understand the fundamental properties, principles, and processes governing molecules and their interactions in materials or chemical systems to provide the scientific foundation to create revolutionary capabilities for the future warfighter, such as new protective and responsive materials, sensors, and munitions.

Polymer Chemistry explores the molecular-level link between polymer microstructure, architecture, functionality, and macroscopic properties. In the long term, research in this area will provide the foundation to enable the design and synthesis of functional polymeric materials that give the Soldier new and improved protective and sensing capabilities as well as capabilities not yet imagined.

(i) Precision Polymeric Materials explores new approaches for synthesizing polymers with precisely defined molecular weight, microstructure (monomer sequence and tacticity), branching, and functional group location, and on using self assembly to create precise, complex polymer structures with diverse functions and new properties.

(ii) Mechano-responsive Polymeric Materials focuses on the design and synthesis of novel polymers that undergo predictable conformational and/or chemical changes in response to specific external stimuli. Mechanochemistry, self-immolative polymers, and

reconfigurable materials are of particular interest. Research in this area is coordinated with complementary studies funded through ONR.

(iii) Photoreactive Polymers focuses on the design and synthesis of polymers that have predetermined responses to electromagnetic energy. The Extramural Basic Research Campaign follows AFRL research in this area, as AFRL has made significant investments in photorefractive polymer design that may lead to the development of materials for active holographic displays for real-time battlefield surveillance from space.

Molecular Structure and Dynamics drives studies to understand state-selected dynamics of highly energetic reactions of molecules in gas and condensed phases across a wide variety of conditions and to develop theories that are capable of accurately describing, predicting, and harnessing these phenomena. In the long term, these studies may serve as the basis for the design of future propellants and explosives that are more efficient to produce, more effective in the field, and safer for transport.

(i) Molecular Dynamics broadly supports research on the study of energy transfer mechanisms in molecular systems (reactive and non-reactive). The Extramural Basic Research Campaign leads research in this area and also collaborates with AFOSR and DARPA efforts, including studies of femtosecond molecular dynamics and ultrafast laser science and engineering. Unique spectroscopic capabilities are expected to result from this program especially in the areas of attosecond sources of electromagnetic radiation.

(ii) Quantitative Theoretical Methods supports research to develop and validate theories for quantitatively describing and predicting the properties of chemical reactions and molecular phenomena in gas and condensed phases.

(iii) Condensed Phase Chemistry of Explosives explores the fundamental chemical phenomena that occur at the instance that a material absorbs a stimulus, which are key to the material's sensitivity and explosive performance properties. Understanding the detailed chemistry of such phenomena is vital to finding and creating new materials with improved properties. The Extramural Basic Research Campaign follows the work of the Joint Munitions Program of DoE and DoD.

Electrochemistry drives studies to understand and control reactant activation and electron transfer and how these are coupled with electrode, catalysis, electrolyte, and interface. These studies provide the foundation for developing advanced power generation and storage technology.

(i) Reduction-Oxidation (RedOx) Chemistry and Electrocatalysis seeks to discover new spectroscopic and electrochemical techniques for probing surfaces and selected species on those surfaces and the RedOx chemistries of those species. The Extramural Basic Research Campaign leads research in this area, while collaborating with AFOSR in the subfield of biological electrochemistry.

(ii) Transport of Electroactive Species seeks to uncover the mechanisms of transport through polymers and electrolytes, design tailorable electrolytes based on new polymers and ionic liquids, and also explore new methodologies and computational approaches to study the selective transport of species in charged environments.

(iii) Corrosion research aims to uncover the mechanisms of corrosion for the protection of materiel. The Extramural Basic Research Campaign follows research led by ONR in this area.

Reactive Chemical Systems seeks to obtain a molecular-level understanding of interfacial activity and of dynamic nanostructured and self-assembled chemical systems. In the long term, research in this area will enable the design and synthesis of new chemical systems that may provide unprecedented hazardous materials management capabilities and Soldier survivability.

(i) Interfacial Activity efforts are on understanding the mechanisms of mass transport and reactivity on surfaces and at interfaces as well as how to control the structure and function of chemical and biological molecules on surfaces. The Extramural Basic Research Campaign collaborates with ECBC in studies of metal-organic frameworks (MOFs), a subset of this research area. Collaborative work includes the development, funding, and review of research to understand the fundamental properties of MOFs that control adsorption, mass transport, and reactivity.

(ii) Synthetic Molecular Systems is exploring novel methods for incorporation of multi-functionality, dynamic and responsive behavior into chemical systems, including the stabilization of nanostructured and self-assembled systems, incorporation of enhanced catalytic activity into chemical systems, and the design and synthesis of chemical systems that sense and respond to specific external stimuli.

(iii) Nanoscale Building Blocks explores nanoscale structures, such as quantum dots, nanoscale clusters, and inorganic cage structures, as potential building blocks for materials with novel properties. The Extramural Basic Research Campaign follows the extensive AFOSR efforts in this area.

EXTRAMURAL BASIC RESEARCH CAMPAIGN's Chemical Sciences S&T Footprint	
S&T AREA	**POSTURE**
Precision Polymeric Materials	LEAD
Mechano-responsive Polymeric Materials	COLLABORATE
Photoreactive Polymers	WATCH
Molecular Dynamics	COLLABORATE
Quantitative Theoretical Methods	LEAD
Condensed Phase Chemistry of Explosives	WATCH
Reduction-Oxidation (RedOx) Chemistry and Electrocatalysis	COLLABORATE
Transport of Electroactive Species	LEAD
Corrosion	WATCH
Interfacial Activity	COLLABORATE
Synthetic Molecular Systems	LEAD
Nanoscale Building Blocks	WATCH

LIFE SCIENCES is focused on basic research to discover, understand, and exploit biological systems that are expected to create revolutionary capabilities for the Army of 2030 and beyond. Discoveries in this area are expected to lead to capabilities in materials and Soldier performance augmentation, well beyond the limits facing today's Army.

Life Sciences (Biological Sciences) supports research to discover and understand the underlying properties, principles, and mechanisms governing DNA, RNA, proteins, organelles, cells, organisms, multi-species interactions, and neurological and cognitive systems, that in the long term are expected to lead to new methods for creating new biomaterials, sensing and inactivating toxins, optimizing warfighter physical and mental performance capabilities, and a range of revolutionary applications to protect the Soldier.

Genetics is focused on discoveries and characterization mechanisms and factors that influence DNA stability and mutagenesis, gene expression, and genetic regulatory pathways in prokaryotes, eukaryotes, and eukaryotic organelles. This includes studies to understand genetic instability at a population level, mitochondrial regulation and biogenesis, oxidative phosphorylation, oxidative stress, and the interactions and communication between the mitochondria and the nucleus. In addition, this area develops an empirical understanding of general mechanisms by which genomic, transcriptomic, and proteomic components respond to alterations in the population-genetic environment.

(i) DNA Instability seeks to understand the forces that determine the rate and range of prokaryotic genetic change and to identify key genetic regulators and critical human polymorphisms in biochemical pathways critical to human protection and performance. The Extramural Basic Research Campaign leads research in this area, while also collaborating with the Defense Forensic Science Center, the FBI, and other agencies to develop new methods to understand the environmental influence of mutation patterns in prokaryotes.

(ii) Stress aims to identify, characterize, and modulate genetic pathways and molecular cascades to determine whether responses to stress or trauma are productive or counterproductive. The Extramural Basic Research Campaign leads research in this area, while also collaborating with complementary NIH and DARPA efforts.

(iii) Regeneration explores genetic and physiological mechanisms through which certain species regenerate, and how potential homologous mechanisms in humans could be controlled. The Extramural Basic Research Campaign collaborates with and follows the work of MEDCOM-MRMC and NIH in this area.

Neurosciences drives non-medically oriented studies to elucidate the fundamental physiology underlying perception, cognition, learning, and neuro-motor output. This includes the perceptual and/or psycho-physiological implications of mind-machine interfaces ranging from optimizing auditory, visual and/or somatosensory display and control systems based on physiological or psychological states through modeling of individual cognitive dynamics and decision making.

(i) Multisensory Synthesis aims to understand how the human brain functions in relation to the interaction of sensory, cognitive and motor processes during its performance of real-world tasks. Research focuses on mapping, quantifying and modeling distributed neural processes that mediate these features to ultimately develop better understanding of cognition for eventual application to Soldier performance.

(ii) Neuronal Computation is focused on understanding how living neuronal circuits generate desirable computations, affect how information is represented, show robustness to damage, incorporate learning and facilitate evolutionary change. Cell culture, brain slice and *in vivo* models are used to develop better understanding of living neural networks for eventual application in Army systems. The Extramural Basic Research Campaign leads research in this area, while collaborating with DARPA in technology development and analytical tools that will enable basic research in brain- and neuromuscular-interfaces that are expected to deliver more efficient human-machine interaction.

(iii) Novel Bio-sensing Strategies seeks to understand neurophysiological mechanisms involved in long distance navigation capabilities. The Extramural Basic Research Campaign follows AFOSR research in this area, which includes studies of bio-mediated

methods for magnetic field detection by avian neural systems. These studies could lead to greater understanding of biomimetic approaches for improved situational awareness.

Biochemistry focuses on elucidation of mechanisms and forces underlying the function, structure, and organization of biological molecules. Fundamental mechanistic understanding of biomolecular processes is also utilized to engineer biomolecular systems to control activity, specificity and spatial organization. These studies may ultimately enable the design and development of novel materials, molecular sensors, and nanoscale machines that exploit the exceptional capabilities of biomolecules.

(i) Biomolecular Specificity and Regulation aims to understand how biomolecules recognize and interact with their targets, as well as how biomolecules are activated or inhibited, leading to approaches to modulate and control biomolecular activity through protein engineering approaches. The Extramural Basic Research Campaign leads research in this area, while collaborating with complementary research funded through NSF and NIH.

(ii) Biomolecular Assembly and Organization aims to explore the fundamental principles governing biological self-assembly, to understand and control the interactions and forces operating at the interface between biological molecules and abiological materials, and to identify innovative approaches to support biological activity outside of the cellular environment. The Extramural Basic Research Campaign leads research in this area, while collaborating with complementary research funded through ONR and NSF.

(iii) Synthetic Biology explores methods and mechanisms to harness organisms or biological systems to perform engineering tasks typically impractical with conventional methods. This area has significant potential to impact nearly every aspect of society including medicine, food, chemicals, materials, energy, and agriculture. To achieve the challenging goals of predictable and controlled engineering of biology, significant coordinated investments are required, and the Extramural Basic Research Campaign collaborates with ONR and DARPA on basic and applied research in this area.

(iv) Bionanocombinatorics research is an emerging area that aims to use combinations of positionally encoded biomolecules and inorganic nanostructures to create materials and devices with unique properties or functions. The Extramural Basic Research Campaign is following AFOSR research in this area to assess the potential of this new research area and to determine how to effectively leverage results for Army programs.

Microbiology explores the physiology, genetics, ecology, intercellular interactions, and adaptation of microbes, including viruses, prokaryotes, and single-celled eukaryotes. Microbes serve as a model system to explore a variety of fundamental questions that are too complex or costly to study effectively in multi-cellular organisms.

(i) Intercellular Dynamics aims to discover and map the genetic, proteomic, and metabolic mechanisms involved in bacterial and fungal intercellular communication. This includes studies to understand and ultimately control the community aspects of bacteria and fungi, such as quorum sensing, host-pathogen/symbiont interactions, strain emergence, programmed cell death, and interactions in mixed populations. In addition to leading research in this area the Extramural Basic Research Campaign collaborates with and follows complementary studies funded through NSF and NIH.

(ii) Microbial and Viral Adaptation focuses on understanding how individual bacteria, fungi, and viruses adapt at the molecular level and macroscale. This area includes studies of viral infection and replication mechanisms and microbial stress resistance. The Extramural Basic Research Campaign leads research in this area, while collaborating with

NSRDEC in the subfield of spore germination mechanisms. In addition, ARL follows MEDCOM-MRMC's initiatives to identify eukaryotic transcriptional patterns indicative of pre-symptomatic exposure to biological threat agents.

(iii) Microbial Targets for Drug Development seeks to understand the genetic and metabolic dynamics of microbial growth and adaptation with the goal of discovering potential targets for drug design. In addition, new drugs such as enzymatic inhibitors, once validated, often provide a new tool to better characterize these pathways. The Extramural Basic Research Campaign chiefly follows the work of MEDCOM-MRMC, NSF, NIH, CDC, and industry in this research area.

EXTRAMURAL BASIC RESEARCH CAMPAIGN's Life Sciences (Biological Sciences) S&T Footprint	
S&T AREA	**POSTURE**
DNA Instability	COLLABORATE
Stress	COLLABORATE
Regeneration	WATCH
Multisensory Synthesis	LEAD
Neuronal Computation	COLLABORATE
Novel Bio-sensing Strategies	WATCH
Biomolecular Specificity and Regulation	COLLABORATE
Biomolecular Assembly and Organization	COLLABORATE
Synthetic Biology	COLLABORATE
Bionanocombinatorics	WATCH
Intercellular Dynamics	COLLABORATE
Microbial and Viral Adaptation	COLLABORATE
Microbial Targets for Drug Development	WATCH

Life Sciences (Social Sciences) explores human behavior at the individual, local, and state levels, with the long-term goal of predicting, detecting, and influencing decisions and activities that impact U.S. interests and national security.

Cultural and Behavioral Science seeks to gain a better understanding of human behavior through the development of mathematical, computational, statistical, and simulation models that provide fundamental insights into factors contributing to human socio-cultural dynamics. The research involves a wide range of approaches, including computational and mathematical modeling, agent-based simulations, econometric and statistical modeling. Since building and validation of models in the social sciences is often limited by the availability of adequate and appropriate sources of primary data, some of the supported research includes collection of primary data for the development and testing of models.

(i) Predicting Human Behavior pursues fundamental understanding of human behavior at various levels – from individuals to entire societies – and across various temporal and spatial scales. It includes studies of interactions between human and natural systems, the role of culture and cognition in accounting for variations in human behavior, and human decision-making under risk and uncertainty.

(ii) Complex Human Social Systems includes research on the evolution and dynamics of social systems and organizations, human adaptation and response to both natural and human induced perturbations, the search for organizing principles in social networks,

and the emergent and latent properties of dynamic social systems and networks. *(iii) Natural and Human Systems* aims to understand human systems and their relationships with natural systems, such as climate, ecology, terrain, and natural resources. This work enables development of theoretical models to identify the effects of complex interdependencies between humans, social systems, natural systems, and the effects of those interdependencies on individual and group behavior, as well as broad social patterns. The Extramural Basic Research Campaign collaborates with ONR, AFOSR, the National Oceanic and Atmospheric Administration, and the Office of the Secretary of Defense's Minerva Initiative on advancing basic research and data collection efforts related to human systems and their relationships with natural systems. ARL also follows research in the Department of Energy and NASA in this area.

Institutional and Organizational Science explores emergence, maintenance, and evolution of human organizations and institutions, including but not limited to societies, states, religions, markets, economic systems, legal systems, bureaucracies, political parties, social movements, and formal and informal networks.

(i) Identification of General Theory explores the use of details abstracted from particular social contexts, to be used universally across the globe to anticipate crises or change.

(ii) Data collection and Analysis attempts to make feasible the consistent monitoring of events around the globe. A broad range of approaches include the use of empirical methods that require primary data collection such as random control trials, field experiments, surveys, comparative and observational studies, as well as use of secondary data sources, such as archival data or news reports, and also formal, mathematical or computational approaches. Of special interest is research on the reciprocal effect of individuals on institutions and institutions on people: how do institutions shape attitudes and opportunities and constrain behavior and how do choices and actions of people and groups, impact and change institutions.

(iii) Governance Structures focuses on data collection on the emergence, maintenance, and evolution of political and legal structures. The Extramural Basic Research Campaign collaborates with and follows the Office of the Secretary of Defense's Minerva Initiative basic research program in this area.

Social Informatics quantifies technology-based social interaction phenomena, to develop metrics for the quantified phenomena, and to develop forensic and predictive analytical and computational models based on these quantifications and metrics.

(i) Quantification and Metrics focuses on the extraction of information from social media and requires the quantification of and metrics for these phenomena

(ii) Analytical and Computational Models focuses on analytical and computational models for both forensic and predictive purposes. These models complement the qualitative models of much of sociological research, especially those in the less-investigated area of weak-tie sociology that is important for technology-based social interaction.

(iii) Social Health Informatics seeks to assess the links between well-being, performance, healthcare, biomedical breakthroughs, lifestyle choices, social relationships, and social stratification. The Extramural Basic Research Campaign follows research programs in MEDCOM-MRMC, NIH, CDC, and industry in this area. ARL leverages the studies of other organizations to provide new methodologies of analyzing Big Data that informs ARL's basic research directions.

EXTRAMURAL BASIC RESEARCH CAMPAIGN's Life Sciences (Social Sciences) S&T Footprint	
S&T AREA	**POSTURE**
Predicting Human Behavior	COLLABORATE
Complex Human Social Systems	COLLABORATE
Natural and Human Systems	WATCH
Identification of General Theory	COLLABORATE
Data collection and Analysis	COLLABORATE
Governance Structures	COLLABORATE
Quantification and Metrics	COLLABORATE
Analytical and Computational Models	COLLABORATE
Social Health Informatics	WATCH

INFORMATION SCIENCES is focused on basic research to discover, understand, and exploit the mathematical, computational, and algorithmic foundations that are expected to create revolutionary capabilities for the Army of 2030 and beyond. Discoveries in this area are expected to lead to capabilities in materials, the information domain, and Soldier performance augmentation, well beyond the limits facing today's Army.

Computational Sciences is focused on understanding the fundamental principles and techniques governing computational models and architectures for intelligent, trusted, and resilient computing. It provides the foundation for revolutionary capabilities for future warfighters in signal and data processing, data fusion, and social informatics.

Information Processing and Fusion establishes innovative theories for data processing, information extraction, and information integration that give the Soldier new and improved real-time situational awareness and advanced targeting.

(i) Foundations of Image and Multimodal Data Analysis seeks task-oriented representations of multimodal data to enable the understanding of complex, multi-sensor data and their contextual information, explores novel approaches in detection, localization, and recognition of objects, actions, and locations to extract activity-based intelligence, and creates integrated approaches that enable semantic descriptions of objects and events including relations.

(ii) Data and Information Fusion develops advanced mathematical theories and approaches for integrating multimodal data and their contextual information, and establishes systematic and unifying approaches for their fusion from diverse sources and in networked environments.

(iii) Active and Collaborative Sensing creates frameworks to integrate mobility, sensor-selection, modality selection, and active observation for performing real-time assessment, improving sensing performance, and carrying out performance-driven active data collection.

(iv) Artificial Intelligence (AI) based Visual Data Analytics seeks to improve the performance of object recognition and scene understanding that are fundamental to data analysis and information processing. ARL collaborates with ONR in this area of research.

(v) Space Situation Awareness research involves research on data association, tracking, and recognition using multimodal sensor networks that are relevant to information processing and fusion, particularly in collaborative sensing and fusion research.

Computational Architectures and Visualization seeks to discover new architectures, computational methods, and software tools for efficiently simulating and visualizing massive data sets.

(i) Computational Architectures explores computational theories, mathematical abstractions, and models of computation needed to address the difficulties associated with heterogeneous, parallel and distributed processing, to determining how these map onto emerging computational resources of different types including multi-core, quantum, cloud, and chaotic computing.

(ii) Visualization seeks new techniques on making very large simulations and the visualization of massive data sets faster, more computationally efficient, and more interactive for the user while maintaining an appropriate level of fidelity and physical realism for Army situational awareness.

(iii) Approximation Theory is focused on discovering and understanding methodologies to facilitate the reliable approximation of either continuous or partially known functions using the discrete tools available in a computational environment. These methods provide the mathematical basis of computer visualization.

(iv) Image Based Rendering is focused on using photographic imagery as a basis for the computer graphic re-creation through exploration of new lighting models and 3D reconstruction techniques.

Information and Software Assurance develops fundamental principles of robust and resilient systems that can enable sustainment under adversarial conditions. This also enables trustworthy computing and communication, regardless of threat conditions.

(i) Highly Assured Tactical Information seeks fundamental approaches for trustworthy tactical communications and principles and models for robust and resilient tactical information processing.

(ii) Resilient and Robust Information Infrastructure explores cyber situation awareness theory and a framework which combines intrusion prevention, detection, response, and recovery. It establishes fundamental scientific principles for building robust mission-sustaining information systems.

(iii) Software System Security focuses on evaluation methods that identify vulnerabilities in software and techniques that mitigate software errors and loopholes for better assurance.

(iv) Cyber Physical Systems (CPS) research aims to ensure information assurance for systems with computing and communications embedded in objects and structures in the physical world.

EXTRAMURAL BASIC RESEARCH CAMPAIGN's Computational Sciences S&T Footprint	
S&T AREA	**POSTURE**
Foundations of Image and Multimodal Data Analysis	LEAD
Data and Information Fusion	LEAD
Active and Collaborative Sensing	LEAD
Artificial Intelligence (AI) based Visual Data Analytics	COLLABORATE
Space Situation Awareness	WATCH
Computational Architectures	LEAD

Visualization	LEAD
Approximation Theory	COLLABORATE
Image Based Rendering	WATCH
Highly Assured Tactical Information	LEAD
Resilient and Robust Information Infrastructure	LEAD
Software System Security	COLLABORATE
Cyber Physical Systems (CPS)	WATCH

Network Sciences pursues discovery and understanding of robust mathematical principles and laws that govern a broad variety of networks including organic, social, and electronic. These principles and laws serve as the foundation for the creation of algorithms which may be leveraged for autonomous system reasoning.

Multi-agent Network Control seeks to model, analyze, design, and control complex real-time physical and information-based systems – including distributed and embedded; networked; autonomous and semi-autonomous; non-linear; smart structures; and decentralized systems.

(i) Intelligent Control is focused on research directed toward non-traditional approaches to control such as embedded under high uncertainty, clustering, and complex environments.

(ii) Multi-agent Systems is focused on extending the mathematical foundations of distributed system theory – massive-scale, low-cost, highly-distributed agents cooperating over networks in highly uncertain, clustering, and complex environments. In addition, control over emergent behavior for heterogeneous multi-agent systems; accommodative-cooperative-collaborative theory of multi-agent behavior and interaction; and multi-player/ multi-objective game theory understanding is pursued through this effort.

(iii) Dynamics and Control research is focused on better understanding traditional control theory for physical systems, based on the paradigm of sense-decide-control in a single physical, autonomous system.

Social and Cognitive Networks is at the frontiers of mathematics and neuroscience to support timely, robust, near-optimal decision making in highly complex, dynamic systems operating in uncertain, resource-constrained environments.

(i) Mathematical Modeling of Neural Processes combines aspects of actual and artificial neural networks to drive new learning models. The focus is on creating quantitatively modeled decision behaviors in neural-anatomical or other observable measures to explain how factors such as complexity, uncertainty, stressors, social and other dynamics affect warfighter decision making.

(ii) Stochastic Optimization and Modeling is focused on advances in mathematical algorithms that better address stochastic data properties common in highly dynamic, heterogeneous and complex operational environments, and in environments with ill-conditioned and varying information.

(iii) Social Science and Computer Science can be leveraged to synergistically study group decision making to advance understanding of social and cognitive networks.

Communications and Human Networks addresses the fundamental underpinnings of wireless communications and human networking, their similarities, and the interactions between the two. This has many potential Army applications that could include wireless tactical communications, improved command decision-making, and determining the structure of adversarial human networks.

(i) Wireless Communications Networks supports research efforts to discover the fundamental network science principles as they apply to wireless multi-hop communications systems.

(ii) Human Networks seeks to better understand social network structures from heterogeneous data, the structure's effect on decision-making, and the interaction of communications and human networks.

(iii) Adaptive Coding and Modulation for Cognitive Radios in Ad-hoc Networks is focused on exploring techniques to optimize throughput under fading channel conditions. These techniques are being investigated within the contexts of dynamic spectrum allocation and multicast transmission.

(iv) Topological Statistical Modeling seeks to analyze sparse noisy measurement data from complex networks to build accurate network models. These models provide a better understanding of network connectivity and information flow and therefore can be used to predict behaviors and performance of both natural and engineered networks.

Intelligent Networks seeks computable mathematical theories, with attendant analysis of computational complexity, to capture common human activity exhibiting aspects of intelligence.

(i) Integrated Intelligence focuses on the structuring principles that allow synergistic integration of the sub-components of intelligent behavior – including vision, knowledge representation, reasoning, and planning.

(ii) Adversarial Reasoning focuses on combining the elements of Game Theory, knowledge representation, and social sciences, to provide an environment through which to reason about groups/societies in a robust manner.

(iii) Theory of Mind is focused on better understanding cognitive science-based theory centered on how the human mind works.

(iv) Human-Robot Teaming research concentrates on discovery and understanding of methods for facilitate the collaborative teaming of human's and robots for improved human performance.

EXTRAMURAL BASIC RESEARCH CAMPAIGN's Network Sciences S&T Footprint	
S&T AREA	**POSTURE**
Intelligent Control	LEAD
Multi-agent Systems	LEAD
Dynamics and Control	COLLABORATE
Mathematical Modeling of Neural Processes	LEAD
Stochastic Optimization and Modeling	LEAD
Social Science and Computer Science	WATCH
Wireless Communications Networks	LEAD
Human Networks	LEAD
Adaptive Coding and Modulation for Cognitive Radios in Ad-hoc Networks	COLLABORATE
Topological Statistical Modeling	WATCH
Integrated Intelligence	LEAD
Adversarial Reasoning	LEAD
Theory of Mind	COLLABORATE
Human-Robot Teaming	WATCH

Mathematical Sciences underlies and enables understanding of complex nonlinear systems, stochastic networks and systems, mechanistic models of adaptive biological systems and networks, and the vast variety of partial differential equation based phenomena. Nonlinear structures and metrics for modeling and studying complex systems are sought, as is creating theory for the control of stochastic systems, spatial-temporal statistical inference, data classification and regression analysis, predicting and controlling biology through hierarchical and adaptive models, enabling new capabilities through bio-inspired techniques, creating high-fidelity computational principles for sharp-interface flows, solving inverse problems, deriving reduced-order methods, and developing computational linguistics.

> *Modeling of Complex Systems* seeks quantitative models of human-based or hybrid physics and human-based phenomena by identifying basic analytical principles and using human goal-based metrics. The identification of accurate metrics is part of the mathematical framework and is of great interest, as traditional metrics often do not capture the characteristics that are of particular interest to the Army.

> *(i) Geometric and Topological Modeling* seeks representation of complex, irregular geometric objects and of complicated, often high-dimensional abstract phenomena such as urban and natural terrain, geophysical features, biological objects, and information flow.

> *(ii) Small-group Social and Sociolinguistic Modeling* seeks mathematically justified, practically useful, and computationally tractable quantitative models of small social groups and sociolinguistic phenomena inherent in operations, training, and mission planning.

> *(iii) Novel Data Sets for Social Analysis* seeks to assemble a collection of data sets that is minimally large and diverse enough to span the space of all interesting features useful in quantitative social analysis

> *(iv) Big Data of Social Network Analysis* seeks methods to intelligently/efficiently gather, store, search, retrieve, analyze, characterize, and model the massive amount of quantitative data that is now available and of potential value in many. This is a rapidly growing area that is dominated and driven by huge databases and has intense interest by the commercial and intelligence communities.

> *Probability and Statistics* derives innovative theory and techniques in stochastic/statistical analysis and control. These are the foundations for revolutionary capabilities in counter-terrorism, weapon systems development, and network-centric warfare.

> *(i) Stochastic Analysis and Control* creates the theoretical foundation for modeling, analysis, and control of stochastic networks, stochastic infinite dimensional systems, and open quantum systems. This includes random fields and/or stochastic differential equations in finite or infinite dimensions. These efforts underpin many Army modeling, analysis, and control areas.

> *(ii) Statistical Analysis and Methods* creates innovative statistical theory and methods for network data analysis, spatial-temporal statistical inference, system reliability, and classification and regression analysis. This research area supports the Army's need for real-time decision-making under uncertainty, and for the design, testing and evaluation of systems in development.

> *(iii) Multivariate Heavy Tailed Statistics* research is focused on developing algorithms for analysis of anomaly detection and fragment patterns modeling.

> *(iv) Quantum Information Theory* methods and results from infinite dimensional quantum channels that may be applicable to better understanding quantum control.

Biomathematics identifies and formularizes fundamental principles of biological structure, function, and development across biological systems and scales. These studies may enable revolutionary advances in Soldier health, performance, and materiel, either directly or through bio-inspired methods.

(i) Computational Cell and Molecular Biology elucidates and models the fundamental principles by which biological elements such as genes, proteins, and cells are integrated and function as systems.

(ii) Multiscale Modeling/Inverse Problems involves creating mechanistic mathematical models of biological systems at different temporal and/or spatial scales, and synchronizing their connections from one level of organization to another, with the goal of achieving a deeper understanding of biological systems and eventually connecting top-down and bottom-up approaches.

(iii) Fundamental Laws of Biology seeks to find and formularize, the basic and general principles underlying the field of biology.

(iv) Predictive Multiscale Models for Biomedical, Biological, Behavioral, Environmental and Clinical Research involves mechanistic modeling of biological systems using innovative techniques to connect mechanisms at multiple spatial and/or temporal scales.

(v) Neural Activity research seeks to use newly-available data from the broader biomathematical community, methods developed for gathering neural activity data, and experimental results to form and test hypotheses and to validate models in neural activity that can be of benefit to others in this specialized experimental domain to further specific interests in Traumatic Brain Injury (TBI), neural linkages to biochronicity, and other areas.

Computational Analysis develops new mathematical understanding to enable faster and higher fidelity computational methods, as well as new methods that will enable modeling of future problems. This will enable the algorithmic analysis of classes of problems through identifying basic computational principles, structures, and metrics, giving the Army new and improved capabilities in areas such as high fidelity modeling, real-time decision and control, communications, and intelligence.

(i) Multiscale Methods seeks to achieve higher fidelity and more efficient modeling of multiscale phenomena in a variety of media.

(ii) PDE-Based Methods focuses on the mathematics for higher fidelity, more efficient modeling of sharp-interface phenomena, to discover new methods for inverse problems that converge globally, and to create reduced-order methods that achieve sufficiently accurate yet much more efficient solutions.

(iii) Computational Linguistics focuses on creating a new understanding of natural language communication and translation through new concepts in structured modeling.

(iv) High Performance Computing (HPC) seeks to develop advanced architectures, innovative computational algorithms that can take advantage of those architectures, and associated tools to help DoD scientists model, solve, and engineer solutions to complex problems.

(v) Biomimetic Computing seeks to find new methods of analog computation that mimic some of the many ways that nature and biology perform complex computations, such as reaction-diffusion computing soups, route planning by avians, and human ability to quickly decode complex acoustic and visual signals

EXTRAMURAL BASIC RESEARCH CAMPAIGN's Mathematical Sciences S&T Footprint	
S&T AREA	POSTURE
Geometric and Topological Modeling	LEAD
Small-group Social and Sociolinguistic Modeling	LEAD
Novel Data Sets for Social Analysis	COLLABORATE
Big Data of Social Network Analysis	WATCH
Stochastic Analysis and Control	LEAD
Statistical Analysis and Methods	LEAD
Multivariate Heavy Tailed Statistics	COLLABORATE
Quantum Information Theory	WATCH
Computational Cell and Molecular Biology	LEAD
Multiscale Modeling/Inverse Problems	LEAD
Fundamental Laws of Biology	LEAD
Predictive Multiscale Models for Biomedical, Biological, Behavioral, Environmental and Clinical Research	COLLABORATE
Neural Activity	WATCH
Multiscale Methods	LEAD
PDE-Based Methods	LEAD
Computational Linguistics	LEAD
High Performance Computing (HPC)	COLLABORATE
Biomimetic Computing	WATCH

ENGINEERING SCIENCES is focused on basic research to discover, understand, and exploit new material systems, mechanical systems, electronics, and photonics that are expected to create revolutionary capabilities for the Army of 2030 and beyond. Discoveries in this area are expected to lead to capabilities in materials, the sciences for maneuver, the information domain, the sciences of lethality and protection, and Soldier performance augmentation, well beyond the limits facing today's Army.

Material Sciences seeks to understand the fundamental relationships that link chemical composition, microstructure, and processing history with resultant material properties and behavior.

Materials by Design seeks to establish the experimental techniques and theoretical foundations needed to facilitate the hierarchical design and bottoms-up assembly of multifunctional materials that will enable the implementation of advanced materials concepts including transformational optics, biomimetics, and smart materials.

(i) Directed 3D Self-Assembly of Materials is aimed at enabling the directed 3D assembly of reconfigurable materials, and developing viable approaches to the design and synthesis of multi-component materials incorporating hierarchical constructs.

(ii) Functional Integration of Materials focuses on demonstrating the predictive design and integration of functional properties into complex multi-component systems, and developing analytical techniques for interrogating the evolution of the 3D structure and properties of material assemblies at the nanoscale.

(iii) Optoelectronics and Photonics is focused on exploring new fundamental concepts in photonics, improving the fundamental understanding of photonic devices and components, and enabling discovery and innovation in advancing the frontier of nanophotonics and

associated nanoscience and nanotechnology.

(iv) Electromagnetic Materials develops advanced electronic and magnetic materials critical to the advancement of electronic and magnetic devices. Included are III-V semiconductors, oxides, multi-ferroic and multi-functional materials, magnetic films and materials that address micro-scale thermal management, integration and/or novel functionality

Mechanical Behavior of Materials seeks to reveal underlying design principles and exploit emerging force-activated phenomena in a wide range of advanced materials to demonstrate unprecedented mechanical properties and complementary behaviors.

(i) Force-Activated Materials involves demonstration and characterization of robust mechanochemically adaptive materials based on force-activated molecules and force-activated reactions, tailoring the deformation and failure mechanisms in materials to mitigate the propagation of intense stress-waves and control energy dissipation, and the creation of a new class of adaptive structural materials that demonstrate "mechanical homeostasis."

(ii) Mechanical Complements in Materials is focused on discovery of superior ionic transport materials and transparent materials through a complementary, interdependent, optimization of mechanical properties, investigation of fiber precursors – tailored for lateral and axial interactions to generate new paradigms for revolutionary structural fibers, and validation of new atomic-scale strengthening mechanisms governing bulk mechanical behavior.

(iii) Multifunctional Materials and Microsystems is focused on establishing safer, more maneuverable aerospace vehicles and platforms with unprecedented performance characteristics; and to bridge the gap between materials science and structural engineering to form a science base for materials development and integration criteria.

(iv) Computer Aided Materials Design focuses on alloys, superconducting materials, new polymer composites, high-temperature materials, enhanced capacitors and batteries, and anti-fouling materials relevant to power and energy.

(v) Natural Materials and Systems is focused on the study, use, mimicry, or manipulation of mechanisms used by living systems accomplish their natural functions. While mimicry is a focus of this effort, enhancing the capabilities of organisms for more precise control over their material production is also a goal.

Physical Properties of Materials seeks to elucidate fundamental structural and physical mechanisms responsible for achieving extraordinary electronic, photonic, magnetic and thermal properties in advanced materials to enable future Army relevant innovations.

(i) Free-standing 2D Materials focuses on the creation of novel free-standing 2D materials and heterostructures with physical properties complementary or superior to graphene, and the development of novel characterization techniques specific to 2D materials to determine electronic, photonic, magnetic, and thermal properties.

(ii) Defect Science and Engineering studies the specific influence of structural defects on the physical properties of novel functional materials, and elucidates defect control mechanisms during thin film growth of novel functional materials.

(iii) Low Density Materials is focused on transformative, basic research in materials design and processing to enable radical reductions in system weight with concurrent enhancements in performance and function.

(iv) 2D Materials and Devices beyond Graphene focus is to grow, characterize and understand hetero-structures of different 2D materials with unique electronic, photonic, thermal and structural characteristics. The effort also seeks to design, fabricate and explore devices based on such 2D hetero-structures.

Synthesis and Processing of Materials seeks to discover and illuminate processing-microstructure-property scientific linkages for optimal creation of superior bulk nanostructured materials.

(i) Stability of Nanostructured Materials focuses on the creation of thermally-stable, ultrahigh strength nanocrystalline materials through interfacial grain boundary engineering, and the realization of high strength, stable nanostructured alloys via pinning nano-precipitates and internal coherent boundaries.

(ii) Manufacturing Process Science is focused on discovery of the fundamental physical laws and phenomena of materials processes, and the exploitation of unique phenomena that occur under extreme processing conditions for the creation of advanced materials.

(iii) Alloys and Joining aims to design an alloy to possess optimal mechanical properties for a particular application, and the highest corrosion resistance, with the lightest weight. Research supported in this program focuses closely on the physics, chemistry and materials science of welds to understand the origins of bonding strength and adhesion between different joined substances.

(iv) Bulk Nanostructured Materials takes advantage of the unusual properties of nanomaterials to build hybrid structural materials as combinations or composites of both nanoscale and bulk materials to obtain new materials with enhanced properties compared to the original constituents.

EXTRAMURAL BASIC RESEARCH CAMPAIGN's Material Sciences S&T Footprint	
S&T AREA	**POSTURE**
Directed 3D Self-Assembly of Materials	LEAD
Functional Integration of Materials	LEAD
Optoelectronics and Photonics	COLLABORATE
Electromagnetic Materials	COLLABORATE
Force-Activated Materials	LEAD
Mechanical Complements in Materials	LEAD
Multifunctional Materials and Microsystems	COLLABORATE
Computer Aided Materials Design	COLLABORATE
Natural Materials and Systems	WATCH
Free-standing 2D Materials	LEAD
Defect Science and Engineering	LEAD
Low Density Materials	COLLABORATE
2D Materials and Devices beyond Graphene	COLLABORATE
Stability of Nanostructured Materials	LEAD
Manufacturing Process Science	LEAD
Alloys and Joining	COLLABORATE
Bulk Nanostructured Materials	WATCH

Mechanical Sciences advances the Army and Nation's knowledge and understanding of the fundamental properties, principles, and processes involved in fluid flow, solid mechanics, chemical reacting flows, explosives and propellants, and the dynamics of complex systems of relevance to the Army and the DoD.

Solid Mechanics develops physically-based tools for the quantitative prediction, control, and optimization of Army systems subjected to extreme battlefield environments.

(i) Multiscale Mechanics of Heterogeneous Solids seeks to extend the design envelope of current and future Army structures for predictive continuum damage and cohesive models with a physical basis that is supported by computational modeling and experiments at the appropriate length and time scales.

(ii) Low stiffness, non-linear materials and material systems focuses on the understanding of response and failure of low-stiffness and non-linear materials, including biologic tissues, under dynamic high strain-rate loading.

(iii) Structural Health and Prognosis focuses on developing fundamental understandings required to design and manufacture new materials and structures and to predict their performance and integrity based on mechanics principles.

(iv) Low Density and Structural Lightweight Materials focuses on basic research in materials design and processing to enable radical reductions in system weight with concurrent enhancements in performance and function.

(v) Blast Loading of Panels focuses on developing an understanding of damage and failure of structural panels subjected to cyclic and blast loading.

Complex Dynamics and Systems develops mathematical methods and physical constitutive principles to enable deliberate manipulation and exploitation of dynamic phenomena in very high-dimensional and forcefully maintained nonequilibrium systems spanning the molecular to macroscopic length scales.

(i) Nonequilibrium Dynamical Systems is focused on methods for analyzing, influencing, and engineering high-dimensional dynamics; changes in free-energy, entropy production, and inertia; and dynamic load transfer, interaction, and dissipation within spatially extended physical and engineered systems, highly compliant active structures, and nonergodic heat engines.

(ii) Morphologically Modulated Dynamics is focused on developing principles underlying the efficiency of information processing, control, and energetic transformation on the intricate coupling with, and exploitation of, a physical system's shape, topological structure , and nonlinear dynamics.

(iii) Dynamics and Controls focuses on adaptive control and decision making for coordinated autonomous/semi-autonomous aerospace vehicles in uncertain, information rich, dynamically changing, and networked environments.

(iv) Physics of Living Systems emphasizes the physical principles of organization and function of living systems, including the exploration of artificial life forms.

Propulsion and Energetics exploits recent developments in kinetics and reaction modeling, spray development and burning, and understanding of extraction and conversion of stored chemical energy to enable higher performance propulsion and energetic systems, improved combustion models for engine design, and higher energy density materials, insensitive materials, and tailored energy release rate.

(i) Hydrocarbon Combustion is focused on developing kinetic models for heavy hydrocarbon fuels, novel kinetics model reduction methods, surrogate fuel development,

and research into sprays and flames, especially ignition in high pressure low temperature environments.

(ii) Energetics focuses on novel material performance via materials design, development, and characterization, and investigations into understanding material thermo-mechanical sensitivity.

(iii) Energy Conversion is focused on better understanding the energy needs for operating propulsion systems and their supporting sub-systems.

(iv) Energetic Material Synthesis is focused on exploring improved performance with acceptable insensitivity characteristics for explosives, propellants and reactive materials.

Fluid Dynamics is concerned with the accurate prediction and control of flowfields around maneuvering Army weapon systems.

(i) Unsteady Separation / Dynamic Stall is focused on the prediction and control of unsteady flow separation under realistic flow conditions (high Reynolds number).

(ii) Vortex Dominated Flows seeks the methodology to predict vortex wake development on reasonable computational meshes, and to explore disruption/augmentation of large coherent structures via novel control approaches that affect energy transfer on the viscous dissipation/Kolmogorov scale.

(iii) Flow Interactions and Control focuses on the characterization, modeling/prediction, and control of flow instabilities, turbulent fluid motions, and fluid structure interactions for both bounded and free-shear flows with application to aero-optics, surfaces in actuated motion, flexible and compliant aerodynamic surfaces, vortical flows, and flows with novel geometric configurations.

(iv) Air Vehicle Technology focuses on developing enhanced performance, maneuverability, and survivability of air vehicles with reduced operating and support cost.

EXTRAMURAL BASIC RESEARCH CAMPAIGN's Mechanical Sciences S&T Footprint	
S&T AREA	**POSTURE**
Multiscale Mechanics of Heterogeneous Solids	LEAD
Low stiffness, non-linear materials and material systems	LEAD
Structural Health and Prognosis	COLLABORATE
Low Density and Structural Lightweight Materials	WATCH
Blast Loading of Panels	WATCH
Nonequilibrium Dynamical Systems	LEAD
Morphologically Modulated Dynamics	LEAD
Dynamics and Controls	COLLABORATE
Physics of Living Systems	WATCH
Hydrocarbon Combustion	LEAD
Energetics	LEAD
Energy Conversion	COLLABORATE
Energetic Material Synthesis	COLLABORATE
Unsteady Separation / Dynamic Stall	LEAD
Vortex Dominated Flows	LEAD
Flow Interactions and Control	COLLABORATE
Air Vehicle Technology	COLLABORATE

Electronics seeks materials and novel structures providing new pathways for the design and fabrication of electronic devices with properties that cannot be realized with current technology.

Electromagnetics research focuses on novel active and passive devices and components with improved dynamic range, linearity, bandwidth, and loss performance to give the Soldier enhanced communications , command and control, reconnaissance, surveillance, target acquisition, and weapons guidance and control.

(i) Electromagnetics and Antennas includes coupling of EM radiation into and out of complex structures, electromagnetic wave propagation modeling, and unusual effects in small gaseous plasmas.

(ii) Discovery-Enabled New RF Circuit Concepts leverages hybrid integration of electronic, spintronic, photonic, phononic, and other multi-modal effects of RF circuitry including the exploitation, management, and simulation of non-linear effects.

(iii) Quantum Electromagnetic and Radio Frequency (EM&RF) focuses on the emerging field of quantum RF including entanglement of microwave fields and mechanical oscillators and single photon microwave sources.

(iv) Plasma Electronics is focused on exploiting experiment, theory, and simulation to examine the modification of atmospheric gas density profiles with femtosecond laser pulses and explores the scientific underpinnings of applications to long range, high power waveguiding and laser-induced high voltage discharges.

(v) Graphene Research involves growth and fabrication technologies of this unique material that, when coupled with improved understanding of the critical underlying physical properties, will enable novel device concepts, including ultrafast field-effect transistors and tunable acoustic resonators, which can generate or modify sounds by enhancing selected frequencies.

Nano- and Bio- Electronics studies biological and nanoscale electronic phenomena and processes to create innovative electronic device concepts with unprecedented capabilities and performance, at reduced size, weight, and power.

(i) Nanoelectronic Engineering Sciences focuses on nano-devices and molecular-level electronics, and addresses design, modeling, fabrication, testing and characterization of novel electrically and magnetically-controlled electronic structures.

(ii) Bio-electronics is focused on investigating new mechanisms to interface with and manipulate molecular and biological systems and explores biomimetic approaches to new electronic circuit functionality based on the detailed understanding of biological electrical and magnetic phenomena.

(iii) 2D Material Integration is focused on exploiting the exotic properties of engineered two-dimensional materials by incorporation unique structures with diverse materials to create enhanced functionality and performance.

(iv) Hybrid Nano-CMOS is focused on creating advances in high K FETs and leakage current reduction at the nano-scale to continue to decrease the size as well as capacitance and switching times of silicon-based transistor devices.

EXTRAMURAL BASIC RESEARCH CAMPAIGN's Electronics S&T Footprint	
S&T AREA	**POSTURE**
Electromagnetics and Antennas	LEAD
Discovery-Enabled New RF Circuit Concepts	LEAD
Quantum Electromagnetic and Radio Frequency (EM&RF)	COLLABORATE
Plasma Electronics	COLLABORATE
Graphene Research	WATCH
Nanoelectronic Engineering Sciences	LEAD
Bio-electronics	LEAD
2D Material Integration	COLLABORATE
Hybrid Nano-CMOS	WATCH

Photonics is focused on enhancing the control of generation, emission, transmission, guidance, modulation, signal processing, switching, amplification, and detection of light in both semiconductor and dielectric materials. It is the foundation for new sensing, communication, and power applications for the Soldier.

Optics and Fields involves manipulation of light and the formation of light in extreme conditions.

(i) Extreme Light includes ultra-high intensity light, light filamentation, and femtosecond/attosecond laser physics. Research is needed to better understand how matter behaves under these conditions, and for development of methodologies for extreme light generation and its effective utilization. Potential long-term applications of these pulses include imaging through opaque materials, laser pulse modulation, "observing" electron dynamics, and even controlling electron dynamics. The Extramural Basic Research Campaign leads research in this area, while collaborating with AFOSR in the subfield of high-intensity light interactions with matter.

(ii) Meta-optics is focused on studies of optical angular momentum beams, interaction with and overcoming losses in metamaterials, and the resulting novel optical physics. Cloaking is a well-known possibility of this, but losses and dispersion must be overcome.

(iii) Diffractive Optics is focused on exploring the phenomenon of diffraction and its impact on light.

Optoelectronics focuses on discovery and control of nanostructures and heterostructures for generation, detection, guidance, and control of optical/infrared signals in both semiconductor and dielectric materials. Results of this research program are expected to enable the design and fabrication of new optoelectronic devices that give the Soldier high-data-rate optical networks including free space/integrated data links, improved IR countermeasures, and advanced night vision and 3D imaging.

(i) High Speed Lasers and Interconnects focuses on the dynamics of carrier transport and optical emission efficiencies of novel photonic materials and heterostructures as well as nanostructured topologies that enhance radiative carrier recombination and dynamics.

(ii) Ultraviolet and Visible Photonics is focused on increasing the internal quantum efficiency for light emission with new substrates, alloys, and dopants, improving Raman spectroscopy SNR by multiple UV-Vis excitation wavelengths, and achieving microscale multi-color lasing with high efficiency of emission through use of nanostructure topologies.

(iii) Mid-infrared Lasers is focused on increasingdevice efficiency and output power at both eye-safer and MWIR wavelengths and maintaining mode control with power scaling in solid-state/fiber lasers at eye-safer wavelengths.

(iv) High Energy Lasers research is focusing on improving efficiency, propagation, and thermal management of high energy lasers.

(v) Silicon Photonics is focused on overcoming the indirect bandgap of silicon to create silicon-based optoelectronic devices to create synergistic structures that take advantage of the established silicon electronics platform. Structures of interest include modulators, lasers, detectors, and interconnects as well as direct logic circuits.

Photonic Sensing involves novel detector structures, such as superlattice or barrier structures, as well as novel plasmonic effects, for direct conversion of light to charge in photonic materials and structures.

(i) Absorption is focused on novel electron-photon coupling using plasmonic light compressors, vertical nanowires and pyramids that create light guiding effects, and narrow-band filters using metamaterials.

(ii) Signal to noise enhancements is focused on pursuing novel quantum confinement effects, band structure manipulation, PN junctions at the nano-scale, and novel techniques to combine materials for multi-spectral response. In addition, noise reduction methods are pursued through defect engineering aimed at reducing carrier recombination and novel structures that separate the noise from response.

(iii) Multi Spectral Imaging is focused on creating low cost, high performance, detectors that can distinguish multiple bands in the infrared spectral region. This includes combining disparate material systems in monolithically integrated structures.

(iv) Underwater Acoustic and Magnetic Sensing is focused on investigating piezoelectric and magnetorestrictive effects for acoustic detection and; flux compression, Faraday force, superconducting quantum interference, and innovative pick-up coils for magnetic sensing.

EXTRAMURAL BASIC RESEARCH CAMPAIGN's Photonics S&T Footprint	
S&T AREA	**POSTURE**
Extreme Light	LEAD
Meta-optics	COLLABORATE
Diffractive Optics	WATCH
High Speed Lasers and Interconnects	LEAD
Ultraviolet and Visible Photonics	LEAD
Mid-infrared Lasers	LEAD
High Energy Lasers	COLLABORATE
Silicon Photonics	WATCH
Absorption	LEAD
Signal to noise enhancements	LEAD
Multi Spectral Imaging	COLLABORATE
Underwater Acoustic and Magnetic Sensing	WATCH

COMPUTATIONAL SCIENCES CAMPAIGN

MISSION: To discover, innovate, and transition S&T capabilities that (1) harness the potential of computational sciences and emerging high-performance computers (HPC) to maintain the superiority of Army materiel systems through predictive modeling and simulation technologies; (2) facilitate information dominance, distributed maneuver operations, and human sciences through computational data intensive sciences; and (3) significantly increase and tailor advanced computing architectures and computing sciences technologies on the forefront to enable land power dominance.

VISION: Computational science and the applications of advanced computing technologies will accelerate the United States Army's strategic land power dominance through critical research developments. Strategic and transformative developments in Computational Science will poise the Army of 2030 and beyond as the world's dominant land force. The desired end state is to leverage the full range of S&T enablers to position the Army to excel in distributed operations and increasingly complex operational environments.

COMPUTATIONAL SCIENCES CAMPAIGN PLAN

ARL's S&T investments in Computational Sciences are focused on advancing the fundamentals of predictive simulation sciences, data intensive sciences, computing sciences, and emerging computing architectures to transform the future of complex Army applications. Gains made through these underpinning multidisciplinary research efforts and exploiting emerging advanced computing systems will lead to scientific breakthroughs that are expected to have significant impact on Army materiel systems. Technologies resulting from this multidisciplinary research collaboratively with other ARL S&T campaign innovations will have a significant impact on Power Projection Superiority, Information Supremacy, Lethality and Protection Superiority, and Soldier Performance Augmentation for the Army of 2030.

Computational Sciences uses advanced computing to understand and overcome complex fundamental challenges simultaneous to improving approaches of importance to the Army including weapon systems design; materials-by-design; information dominated and networked battle command applications; system-of-systems analyses; human performance modeling; platform maneuverability; and tactical supercomputers. There are natural synergies among the challenges facing Computational Sciences and ARL's other S&T campaigns. Synergistic advances across all campaigns are expected to enable next generation scientific breakthroughs. The Computational Sciences Campaign heavily relies on ARL's research expertise and facilities devoted to emerging advanced computing architectures, mobile High Performance Computing (HPC), multi-scale and interdisciplinary predictive simulation sciences, multi-dimensional distributed data analytics, and computing sciences. Discoveries and innovations made in this area will exert a significant impact on the Army of the future.

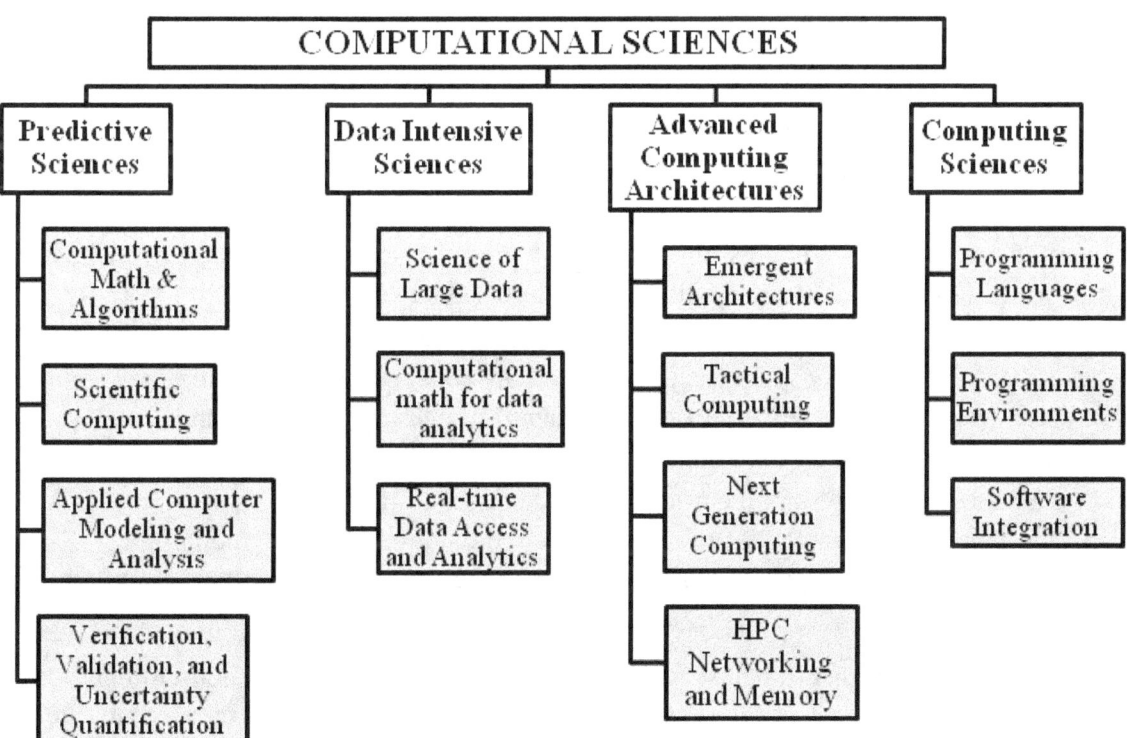

Levels 1 through 3 of the Computational Sciences Campaign Plan Taxonomy

PREDICTIVE SCIENCES concentrates on understanding and exploiting the fundamental aspects of verified and validated computational simulations that predict the response of complex Army systems and guide Army materiel design, particularly in cases where routine experimental tests are extremely difficult to conduct or are infeasible.

Computational Mathematics and Algorithms research encompasses a range of disciplines seeking computational methods to solve fundamental equations. Solutions may be sought for existing equations or new equations may be developed expressly for the purpose of treating problems of Army interest. Problems in which the equations can be expressed in the form of partial differential equations stem from the basic science and engineering disciplines spanning characteristic length scales from sub-atomic to continuum, neural signals, stochastic variables and design theory. Broad classes of problems may also require considerable specialization of solutions based on the platform used to obtain them.

PDE Based Methods encompasses research and development of algorithms and scalable software for solving linear and nonlinear systems, which are often obtained from approximations of partial differential equations (PDE) and arise in numerous areas of science and engineering, including fluid dynamics, structural mechanics, chemistry and materials science, physics, electromagnetic and acoustics, weather modeling, combustion, large scale data mining, and cyber security.

(i) Quantum methods use the most fundamental laws for quantum mechanics to study electronic structure of materials and processes occurring at nano-scale. The QM calculations are computationally very intensive and are necessary to study bond fracture and electronic transitions for physical processes ranging from power-energy, photonic applications to physics, chemistry, and mechanics of high strain rates deformations.

(ii) Atomistic methods are used to study structures and dynamics of materials and processes by considering atoms as the smallest units of matter. The interaction between atoms can be approximated by using more detailed quantum mechanical or experimental, empirical data. Results of atomistic simulations can provide input to the more approximate coarse-graining and also continuum methods.

(iii) Meso-/micro- methods are necessary to conquer temporal and spatial scales beyond the reach of atomistic methods. The processes involving strands, grains or micro-phase separated materials are studied at this level. The long-range effect of defects, interfaces and various failure modes may require use of mesoscale methods.

(iv) Continuum methods are indispensible to study any engineering problems at macroscale. These methods require highest level of model reduction and homogenization. They can access scales necessary to study transport of energy and matter and hydrodynamic as well as manufacturing processes.

(v) Inverse Methods plays unique role in several classes of predictive simulation methodologies. Development of robust inverse optimization and back mapping techniques offers an opportunity to revolutionize discovery and predictions under this research.

Complex Systems consist of many diverse interrelated components coupled through multiple interactions such that the system response cannot be described by a single rule. The systems exhibit emergent response that cannot be predicted by simple combination of the component responses. The systems of interest are highly heterogeneous with a variety of hardware and software elements and possibly a human component.

(i) Computational System Biology involves the use of computer simulations of biological

systems, including cellular subsystems such as the networks of metabolites and enzymes which comprise metabolism, signal transduction pathways and gene regulatory networks, to analyze complex connections of these cellular processes. Applicability of these algorithms to wide class of Army complex systems is of interest.

(ii) Computational Social Sciences exploits advanced computational sciences to pursue interdisciplinary social science, especially large scale complexity modeling, social network analysis, social geographic information systems (GIS), and social simulation models.

(iii) Large Scale Cyber Security/EW/Networks modeling will provide the ability to model with high fidelity, complex military networks for battlefield communication, cyber security, network operations, and the general area of electronic warfare (EW). Modeling networks at different scales and fidelities exploiting advanced computing and computational sciences will enable commanders and analysts to conduct good cyber risk vulnerability analyses and develop robust cyber defenses and operations in real-time or near real-time.

COMPUTATIONAL SCIENCES CAMPAIGN's Computational Mathematics and Algorithms S&T Footprint	
S&T AREA	**POSTURE**
Quantum methods	COLLABORATE
Atomistic methods	LEAD
Meso-micro methods	LEAD
Continuum methods	COLLABORATE
Inverse methods	COLLABORATE
Computational system biology	WATCH
Computational social science	COLLABORATE
Large-scale Cyber/EW/Networks modeling	COLLABORATE

Scientific Computing Research seeks understanding of phenomena that pertain to the scientific pursuits in and across traditional scientific disciplines that lack relevant computational capabilities. Often, the problems are interdisciplinary or require the solution of multiple sets of equations with disparate intrinsic length scales. The equations, algorithms, and conceptual representation, can change with respect to both space and time when traversing scales or crossing the boundaries between scientific disciplines Multi-scale simulations are instrumental in gaining insight into material response predictions; weather and climate forecasting; chemical and biological dispersion; micro-systems; biological ecosystems; and computer and human networks. In each of these areas there is a growing need for higher fidelity computations at the individual scales as well as research into mathematics and computational algorithms bridging the scales.

Multi-scale simulations encompass a range of disciplines where the properties and behavior computed for a limited volume or number of entities is represented as an aggregate response of a significantly greater volume or number of entities. The equations and algorithms, and even the conceptual representation, can change when crossing scales both temporally and spatially.

(i) Atomistic-to-continuum involves computational procedures that cross scales both temporally and spatially. Passing information may require reducing data and representing computational entities as an aggregate response of a significantly greater volume or

number of entities at the more fundamental level. This approach is instrumental in gaining fundamental insight into the behavior of meso-scale and macroscopic entities and also provides an opportunity for macro-scale design that involves manipulation of constitutive elements at atomistic scale.

(ii) Computational Biology is focused on understanding the inherent complexity of interactions among active and passive processes, biology, chemistry, mechanics and other disciplines necessary to describe many fundamental responses underlying system behavior at different spatial and temporal scales. Areas important to the Army include a broad range of neurosciences to traumas and accumulated exposures to physical, chemical and biological environmental factors.

(iii) Battlefield environmental modeling for the Army pertains to detailed nowcast predictions of the atmosphere over short ranges including complex dynamic boundary layer over mission execution battle-space domains in complex terrain areas including urban environments. Prediction of performance of optical, acoustics, and electromagnetic Army materiel systems including particle dispersion under complex atmospheric conditions are essential for Army battlespace engagements.

(iv) Multi-physics methods involve linking variety of disciplines and processes such as shock physics, transport, chemical reactions, interactions with external fields and capabilities to represent stochastic inhomogeneities and account for uncertainty quantification. These processes are critically important for power/energy, electronics, lethality and protection applications as well as to design new materials and manufacturing processes.

(v) Scale bridging involves use of various time acceleration and space embedding methods to reduce the number of degrees of freedom from a model at lower scale to represent phenomena at substantially larger scales.

(vi) System of systems is a set of developing processes, tools, and methods for designing, re-designing and deploying solutions to System-of-Systems challenges. Design for System-of-Systems problems is performed under some level of uncertainty in the requirements and the constituent complex systems, and it involves considerations in multiple levels and domains.

Physical Processes and Mechanisms seeks understanding and exploring mechanisms and physical processes through computational software that are difficult to characterize using experimental and theoretical approaches alone. Often, simulations guide experiments or vice versa in better understanding physics and engineering behind mechanisms or processes. Typically these problems are interdisciplinary and require predictive simulation software.

(i) Interfaces and evolving topologies is focused on defects and other inhomogeneities which determine processes and mechanisms of underlying physics. Evolving topological changes due to external field interactions can be exploited to assist innovations. The treatment of such events often requires stochastic simulations and consideration of an environment.

(ii)Transport and Reactions of energy and matter is of fundamental importance in a number of physical processes and it is often caused by chemical reactions and environmental conditions such as pressure, temperature, voltage, and a difference in a chemical potential. Calculations of reaction kinetics may require use of quantum mechanical methods, diffusion of ions in fuel cells requires atomistic simulations, while fluid dynamics methods may describe combustion processes of propellants. Transport phenomena are critically important in numerous areas of science including batteries,

corrosion, manufacturing, and evolution of explosive reactive products.

(iii) Explosives mechanisms are essential for highly complex lethality research. Research couples chemistry of energetic reactions and shock physics of wave propagation. The outcome of explosive detonation also necessitates large scale modeling in protection, materials studies as well as biological injury and human behavior research.

(iv) High strain and fracture involves investigation of elastic, plastic, and failure behavior of systems. This is a broad field that spans materials and disciplines from mechanical response, to functionality as an electronic component, to biological injury. Plastic flow and failure are often effects of extreme environment such as high strains or ballistic impact.

(v) Multi-functional systems will lead to lighter and versatile solutions for protection, lethality, energy storage, communication, and smart sensor capabilities. Research involves developing an integrated optimized computational-based design methodology. Development of new materials and components with multi-functional capability utilizing physics, chemistry, materials science, manufacturing process simulation, and accurate understanding of interactions between various components is of interest.

(vi) Geometric and Topological Modeling of practical interest are finite collections of manifold elements of different dimensionalities, with boundary incidence as the most important relation among the elements. Adaptive and high-fidelity geometric and topological modeling plays a significant role in predictive modeling.

(vii) Interdisciplinary Mechanisms focuses on the interplay, coupling, understanding, and investigation among disciplines. Fluid-structure-thermal mechanisms, electromagnetic-thermal-structural mechanisms, weapon-target interactions, bio-dispersions in urban terrains, and electronic warfare are of interest.

Emulation methods are dedicated to mimicking the function of hardware by having its low-level functions simulated through software. Emulations are routinely used in computer hardware and software designs. Emulations are emerging as analysis tools for understanding and evaluating non-traditional emulation areas, namely, heterogeneous networks, cyber/EW, brain emulations, quantum, and biological processes.

(i) Algorithms for Emulations focuses on development and associated innovations to impact emerging computing architectures without redesigning algorithms and associated software. Emerging computing architectures are providing a wide class of choices for computational sciences and challenges to computer scientists in developing innovative algorithms.

(ii) Software for Emulations methods can be used in place of simulations for complex system level and physics applications including understanding characteristics of systems, interplay between systems, and exploring physical processes. Non-traditional emulation software application includes quantum, biological, and brain emulations.

(iii) Combined simulations and emulations for parallel discrete event simulations (PDES) will have applicability for modeling of networks, cyber-security, social dynamics, sensor, and complex theory. Development of parallel discrete-event-simulation (PDES) algorithms and numerical methods for using both simulations and emulations concurrently will evolve as a new field of study for complex systems.

COMPUTATIONAL SCIENCES CAMPAIGN's Scientific Computing Research S&T Footprint	
S&T AREA	**POSTURE**
Atomistic-to-continuum	LEAD
Computational biology	COLLABORATE
Battlefield environmental effects modeling	LEAD
Multi-physics methods	COLLABORATE
Scale bridging	COLLABORATE
System of systems	COLLABORATE
Nuero-cognitive modeling	COLLABORATE
Interfaces/evolving topologies	LEAD
Transport & reactions	COLLABORATE
Explosive mechanisms	LEAD
High-strain rate and fracture	LEAD
Multi-functional systems	LEAD
Geometric and topological modeling	WATCH
Interdisciplinary mechanisms	COLLABORATE
Algorithms for emulations	LEAD
Software for emulations	COLLABORATE
Combined simulations and emulations for PDES	COLLABORATE

Applied Computer Modeling and Analysis is focused on using predictive and reliable computational capabilities and tools to impact the design and deployment of critical Army systems and devices. Computational sciences-based enabling tools are required to perform large-scale system analysis from complex model development to detailed analytics.

Large-scale systems and scenarios modeling is focused on modeling high fidelity battle command applications on massively parallel computing systems using integrating desperate software with realistic constraints and boundary conditions.

(i) Modeling devices and systems at full-scale with high-fidelity provides deep insight and dramatically reduces the development time and time to deploy. Similarly, device modeling provides better understanding of physics of individual components and interplay between components.

(ii) High fidelity battle command application takes advantage of emerging computing hardware, predictive software, live-virtual simulations. This approach is expected to provide confidence in decision making and situational awareness across different classes of battle-command applications. Due to complexity of these applications, typically engineering models with significant mathematical assumptions and heuristic approaches are used in for fast running battle command software.

Large-scale computing enablers focuses on predictive software for very large-scale applications requires tools and software for generating input or realistic scenario and tools to post-process enormous amounts of simulation data. These scalable software tools enable large-scale computing.

(i) Adaptive methods for large-scale scenario creation and grid generation concentrates on generation of new scalable mathematical algorithms. High fidelity scenario and mesh generation with all applicable realistic input representations is the first step for large-scale modeling. Error corrections based adaptive input generation methods are essential for

reducing errors and the amount of time devoted to developing problem definition.

(ii) Scalable solvers for large-scale complex modeling require solving systems of equations iteratively for nonlinear applications. These solvers become more complex based on the nonlinearity of the application. Typically, solvers lag behind the rest of the simulations especially for scalability for peta-scale and exa-scale systems.

(iii) Scientific Visualization for multi-scale and multi-physics coupled simulations produce enormous amounts of data on large-scale distributed computing systems. Algorithms and methodologies are needed to accessing, manipulating, and displaying information by taking advantage of human senses and emerging display technologies.

(iv) Imaging methods for scientific computing are emerging as a new field for generating geometric details for simulation models at high fidelity. High-fidelity images provide geometric details necessary for scientific modeling and analysis.

COMPUTATIONAL SCIENCES CAMPAIGN's Applied Computer Modeling and Analysis S&T Footprint	
S&T AREA	**POSTURE**
Modeling devices and systems	COLLABORATE
High fidelity battle command applications	LEAD
Adaptive methods for large-scale scenario and grid generation	COLLABORATE
Scalable Solvers	COLLABORATE
Scientific visualization	LEAD
Imaging methods for scientific computing	COLLABORATE

Verification Validation and Uncertainty Quantification (VVUQ) research is focused on assuring that simulations perform as intended, considering the range of conditions where models and simulations reproduce observed behavior within acceptable tolerances and establishing confidence levels. Army applications span many fields including non-traditional and data intensive sciences and challenges fundamental understanding of VVUQ. The Computational Science Campaign will work with the other ARL Campaigns to explore, develop, and implement VVUQ tools for (i) identifying deficiencies in simulations; (ii) setting guidelines for adequacy of computational results; (iii) exploring the impact of known variability and uncertainty of input; and (iv) control of adaptive algorithms to achieve specified levels of accuracy in solutions.

Verification and validation *are essential for all* simulation applications. Verification is concerned with software verification and solution verification. Validation is concerned with model accuracy assessment, model validity over a range of intended use, and model accuracy.

(i) V&V reusable modules is focused on exploiting new computational approaches, based on reusable modules and knowledge from application domains, to realize robust V&V process and system development.

(ii) Acceptance / adequacy of evaluation methods focus on exploiting a combination of statistical analyses and proper investigation to facilitate the broad acceptance of V&V methods by the user community.

(iii) Runtime V&V supports analyst confidence in performing and understanding complex simulations where real-time sophisticated experimental large-scale data can be taken advantage. Complex and multi-scale simulations are traditionally difficult to V&V. An approach to mitigate this difficulty is by employing run-time V&V techniques to verify the simulation execution trace.

Uncertainty Quantification is concerned with assessment of the level of agreement of a model relative to input and output data, as well as the variation in model results due to various physics, mathematical, and numerical assumptions.

(i) Stochastic Simulation Methods are evolving to understand or quantify uncertainty in simulations. One simple approach is to employ Monte Carlo techniques which replace a single parameter estimate with a sample drawn from the distribution of that parameter. Not only is this approach viable for analytic representations of distributions, but experimentally computed distributions as well.

(ii) Adaptive control of uncertainty focuses on development of nonlinear methods to quantify uncertainty adaptively.

(iii) Uncertainty propagation focuses on better understanding those uncertainties which critically impact the performance of Army systems of interest.

COMPUTATIONAL SCIENCES CAMPAIGN's Verification, Validation and Uncertainty Quantification S&T Footprint	
S&T AREA	**POSTURE**
V&V reusable modules	COLLABORATE
Acceptance / adequacy evaluation methods	COLLABORATE
Run-time V&V	COLLABORATE
Stochastic simulation methods	COLLABORATE
Adaptive control of uncertainty	WATCH
Uncertainty propagation	COLLABORATE

DATA INTENSIVE SCIENCES focuses on understanding and exploiting the fundamental aspects of large-scale, multi-dimensional data analytics. Experiments, observations, and numerical simulations are on the verge of generating petabyte-quantities of data. These massive amounts of data are distributed across disparate locations and pose a challenge in providing real-time analytics that support U. S. military operations.

Science of Large Data research is focused on pursuing theoretical developments and innovations to accommodate high dimensional data and very large-scale sets. These efforts are dedicated to discovering, evolving, and maturing analytic algorithms that efficiently scale to facilitate rapid analyses of massive data sets. The primary goal of this research area is to realize Army-relevant, high accuracy, predictive models based on massive data sets, which take advantage of emerging computing architectures. An additional area of research interest is maturation of methodologies to reduce data set dimensionality prior to modeling; thereby, greatly shortening computational time.

Data Origination is the first step in exploiting computers in solving data science problems is organization of data. Organization of data from different sources is essential for manipulating data.

(i) Large-scale Dynamic Multi-dimensional Heterogeneous Data focuses on the support of the data lifecycle from a high performance computing (HPC) perspective that is critical to the end-to-end scientific discovery and innovation process. Large-scale data is distributed, multi-dimensional, and heterogeneous and requires methodologies for data organization that have deep storage access and sharing in a tightly controlled environment witch support efficient use of high performance distributed computing analytics.

(ii) Scalable Sampling in Experiments and Simulation are essential to support efficient, multi-dimensional spatio-temporal dynamic and very large-scale datasets stored on distributed HPC systems. Sampling is a widely used technique to increase efficiency in data mining applications operating on large organized experimental and simulation data sets.

(iii) Parallel Streaming is widely used to accesses relatively static information to answer evolving and dynamic analytic questions. With stream processing, one can deploy an application that continuously applies analysis to an ever-changing stream of data. Organization of large-scale streaming heterogeneous data is needed for easy access and manipulation on distributed computing for various classes of DoD applications.

(iv) Complex and Evolving Dynamic Data focuses on data structures and algorithms that are required to compute important analytics on rapidly evolving data streams.

(v) High Dimensional Sparse Structured and Unstructured Data focuses on developing scalable algorithms to accommodate nontraditional data types, namely, sparse and dense unstructured high-dimensional data using massively parallel computers.

Scientific mathematics for large-scale data analytics focuses on data mining, machine learning, and pattern recognition methodologies to develop new scalable mathematical approaches.

(i) Evolving or dynamic graphs analytics assumes the structures of the graphs change over time. These temporal dynamics and complexities of very large-scale interactions are critical to model and predict graph changes over time.

(ii) Scalable discrete mathematics is focused on development of discrete event simulations (DES) to realize intuitive and flexible approaches to represent complex systems and associated data.

(iii) Particle Swarm Optimization is focused on computational methods to optimize a problem by iteratively improve a candidate solutions with regard to a given measure of quality, especially in a dynamic discrete environment.

COMPUTATIONAL SCIENCES CAMPAIGN's Science of Large Date S&T Footprint	
S&T AREA	**POSTURE**
Large-scale dynamic multi-dimensional heterogeneous data	LEAD
Scalable Sampling in Experiments and Simulation	COLLABORATE
Parallel streaming	COLLABORATE
Complex evolving dynamic data	COLLABORATE
High-dimensional sparse structured/unstructured data	COLLABORATE
Incomplete data	COLLABORATE
Evolving or dynamic graph analystics	COLLABORATE
Scalable discrete mathematics	COLLABORATE
Particle swarm optimization	COLLABORATE

Computational Methods for Large-scale data analytics research is focused on identifying, evolving, and maturing innovative computational algorithms and methodologies to describe, model, simulate, solve, explore, and optimize control and coordination of computational systems impacted through physical events. Dynamic discrete event systems are data intensive and exist in many technological applications relevant to the Army from communications to system-of-systems to quantum sciences.

Data analytics refers to analyzing large sets of data with the purpose of drawing conclusions and to discover useful information.

(i) Theory/algorithms for numerical and non-numerical analytics are needed for large-scale unstructured numerical data, and non-numerical data analytics. Numerical data can be analyzed using statistical methods, and/or data mining techniques. Non-numerical data is typically multi-modal and unstructured.

(ii) Multisensory-based analytics leverages basic understanding of individual sensory modalities and associated links to multisensory representations and interaction techniques to make the representation and handling of complex data more intuitive and transparent.

Reduced order models research is focused on pursuing new theories, understanding, and interdisciplinary computational methodologies for reducing computational complexity of mathematical models in Army-relevant numerical simulations including underbody blast, brain-structure function, network integration experimentation, and boundary layer atmospheric sciences.

(i) Model order reduction is a technique to project, high-dimensional, state-space onto a properly chosen low-dimensional subspace to generate a smaller system having properties similar to the original system. Complex systems can thus be approximated by simpler systems involving fewer equations and unknown variables, which can be solved quickly.

(ii) Model order reduction for virtual designs is focused on developing virtual design tools utilizing high-dimensional, large scale simulation data for many practical Army applications.

(iii) Multi-dimensional experimental data analytics exploit connections to large-scale simulation data analytics, and similarly compressive measures to adaptively sample deep connections to model reduction.

COMPUTATIONAL SCIENCES CAMPAIGN's Computational Mathematics for Large Data Analytics S&T Footprint	
S&T AREA	**POSTURE**
Theory/algorithms for numerical and non-numerical analytics	COLLABORATE
Multisensory-based analytics	COLLABORATE
Model order reduction	COLLABORATE
Model order reduction for virtual designs	COLLABORATE
Multi-dimensional experimental data analytics	COLLABORATE

Real-time Data Access and Analytics research is focused on exploration of new computing architectures, high-performance networks, and development of "middleware", software components that link high-level data analysis specifications with low-level distributed systems architectures. There is also a major interest in software targeted to end users, to support man-in-the-loop data analyses. Methodologies and techniques developed through this effort are expected to be highly beneficial in large-scale real-time or near real-time data accessing in many scientific disciplines. Army applications of interest include (i) live-virtual-constructive simulations and emulations for C4ISR; (ii) man-in-the-loop simulations for Army ground vehicles; (iii) training solders for cyber vulnerabilities; (iv) integrating computing and measurements for exploring new materials research; (v) cognition experiments feedback.

Mathematical approaches for real-time analytics focuses on the convergence of live simulations, virtual simulations, constructive simulations, gaming simulations, and predictive simulations for training and scientific discoveries.

(i) Accelerated numerical methods are means to support complex model calculations in near-real-time, live-synthetic interactions.

(ii) Live-synthetic simulations focuses on methods that can be used to reduce redundancies in data obtained from live simulations and that must interact with virtual simulations. This effort focuses on efficient methods to reduce the dimension space.

(iii) Enhanced Geometric Algorithms explore highly multi-dimensional data spaces in near real-time. Transformation of large-scale data into information by taking advantage of geometric based fusion approaches are of interest.

Computational methods for real-time large-scale data analytics focuses on development of methodologies specifically designed real-time analyses.

(i) Machine learning based large-scale real-time data analytics focuses on development of methodologies for predictive and real-time large-scale data analytics.

(ii) Multi-level/multi-resolution analytics focuses on methods to facilitate near real-time multi-level querying. Multi-level querying on massively parallel scalable systems will facilitate multi-resolution analytics in real-time for a number of Army applications.

(iii) High fidelity Live-virtual analytics focuses on HPC systems interacting with live entities and providing feedback in real-time through simulations and large-scale data produced by both experiments and simulations.

COMPUTATIONAL SCIENCES CAMPAIGN's Real-time Data Access and Analytics S&T Footprint	
S&T AREA	**POSTURE**
Accelerated numerical methods	COLLABORATE
Live-synthetic simulations	COLLABORATE
Enhanced Geometric Algorithms	WATCH
Machine learning based large-scale real-time data analytics	COLLABORATE
Multi-level/multi-resolution analytics	COLLABORATE
High fidelity Live-virtual analytics	LEAD

ADVANCED COMPUTING ARCHITECTURES concentrates on understanding and exploiting the fundamental aspects of hardware and associated system software for emergent and future computing architectures for mobile, scientific, and data intensive applications. Computing systems include both mobile and fixed/virtual architectures optimized for fast communications, low power consumption, large hierarchical memory, novel and robust algorithms, high resiliency, and HPC networking.

Emergent Computing Architectures research focuses on light weight architectures, large scale on-chip parallelism, and exascale performance to support petascale computing with multi-core processors. These research efforts are also dedicated to developing novel algorithms and application formulations that facilitate the input and output rates required for petascale computing; and application development and performance optimization for next generation computing architectures.

Mobile Computing involves mobile hardware, software, and communications. Exploring mobile computing concept with emerging technologies is expected to provide desired computing architectures for specific Army applications.

(i) Lightweight power aware Architectures research focuses on exploiting low power concepts, multicore networked chips combined with low power heterogeneous computing architectures to realize lightweight and high performance computing architectures.

(ii) Bio-mimetic Computing focuses on using natural exemplars as the basis to develop novel computing architectures.

Scalable Computing is the capability of a computing system to increase its total output under an increased load as computing hardware is added. New developments in computing chip architectures will assist innovations in next generation scalable computer development.

(i) Heterogeneous computing is focused on comparative analyses of computer architectural design and programming systems to realize high performance computer systems.

(ii) Heterogeneous and 3D Architectures focuses on three-D chip integration technologies to achieve energy-centric designs for emerging architectures.

(iii) Many integrated core architectures research is dedicate to efficient methods to integrate hundreds to thousands of small cores, to deliver unprecedented computing performance in an affordable power envelope. Challenges include fine grain power management, memory bandwidth, on die networks, and system resiliency for the many-core integrated systems.

COMPUTATIONAL SCIENCES CAMPAIGN's Emergent Computing Architectures S&T Footprint	
S&T AREA	**POSTURE**
Lightweight Architectures	COLLABORATE
Bio-mimetric computing	WATCH
Heterogeneous computing	LEAD
Heterogeneous 3D Architectures	WATCH
Many integrated core architectures	WATCH

Tactical Computing research is focused on better understanding algorithms and applications which facilitate seamless reach back to large-scale HPC systems and help to supply information to the Soldier at the tactical edge. Research in this area is dedicated to moving beyond optimizing devices in isolation, and embraces the challenges of cross-environment co-design to address the needs of emerging tactical applications.

Tactical HPC Provisioning is focused on providing computer hardware and software infrastructure to the battlespace for improved intelligence and situational awareness for tactical applications.

(i) Tactical Cloudlet research is focused on development of methods to facilitate efficient use of tactical cloudlets and adaptive DoD ad hoc wireless networks.

(ii) Tactical HPC research focuses on heterogeneous, power aware, small footprint, and robust computing architectures, tailored for Army mission command applications.

Computing functionality research focuses on tactical computing architectures for improved size, adaptability, power, performance, and productivity.

(i) Software Driven Adaptable Architectures research focuses on self-adaptive and autonomic computing systems capable of self-configure, healing, optimization, and protection without the need for human intervention.

(ii) Performance, Power, and Productivity research is focused on innovative computing architectural designs for optimizing power, performance, and productivity embodied in a small form factor.

COMPUTATIONAL SCIENCES CAMPAIGN's Tactical Computing S&T Footprint	
S&T AREA	**POSTURE**
Tactical Cloudlet	LEAD
Tactical HPC	LEAD
Software Driven Adaptable Architectures	WATCH
Power, Performance, and Productivity (3P)	COLLABORATE

Next Generation Computing Architectures research is focused on non-traditional computing systems and envisioned to provide disruptive technologies for the Army. Quantum computing, cognitive computing, neuro-synaptic computing, and DNA computing are some emerging concepts.

Very large-scale systems research is focused on peta-scale and above computational capabilities.

(i) Large-scale lightweight multi-core clusters, research is focused on increasing the number of computing cores by orders of magnitude compared to current computing capabilities.

(ii) Exascale Computing research is focused on overcoming the challenges associated with achieving Exascale computing including power, resiliency, networking, parallel programming models, and application software.

Novel Hardware Paradigms focuses on exploring alternatives to Von Neumann computing architectures to enable scientific discoveries and innovations.

(i) Quantum computing is focused on exploiting quantum-mechanical phenomena to realize advanced computing architectures. Integration of millions of devices into one system, producing high-accuracy gates, extending quantum memory lifetimes, processing classical control information, execution of quantum algorithms, and interfacing with quantum network are of interest.

(ii) Neuro-synaptic computing research focuses on using processors that mimic the human brain's computing abilities and power efficiency.

(iii) Social computing systems research is focused on evolving properties that computing systems and systems of people possess together. This understanding will facilitate socially intelligent computing.

(iv) Bio-molecular computing is focused on using DNA, biochemistry, and molecular biology to perform computational calculations involving storing, retrieving, and processing data.

COMPUTATIONAL SCIENCES CAMPAIGN's Next Generation Computing Architectures S&T Footprint	
S&T AREA	**POSTURE**
Large Scale Lightweight Multi-core Clusters	COLLABORATE
ExaScale Computing	WATCH
Quantum computing	WATCH
Social computing systems	WATCH
Neuo-synaptic computing	COLLABORATE
Bio-molecular computing	WATCH

HPC Networking and Memory is focused on fundamental research in next generation networking, memory, and storage for the Army's future computational eco-system. Research areas of particular interest are software defined networking and high-speed optical networking for HPC.

HPC Networking research focuses on addressing networking challenges related to distributed computing.

(i) Software defined networking research focuses on enabling network control to become directly programmable and the underlying infrastructure to be abstracted from applications and network services.

(ii) Distributed Quantum networking focuses on understanding and exploiting distributed quantum computing algorithms over distributed quantum networks.

Computer Memory is focused on understanding and exploiting provision computing. Provision computing, for memory, storage, and efficient movement of data is of interest.

(i) Power aware memory is focused on understanding and exploiting concepts to reduce energy consumption for both embedded and high performance computing systems.

(ii) Racetrack memory research is focuses on understanding and exploiting spin-coherent concepts to realize high density storage concomitant with higher read/write performance.

COMPUTATIONAL SCIENCES CAMPAIGN's HPC Networking and Memory S&T Footprint	
S&T AREA	**POSTURE**
Software defined networking	LEAD
Distributed Quantum networking	COLLABORATE
Power aware memory	WATCH
Race track memory	COLLABORATE

COMPUTING SCIENCES concentrates on understanding and exploiting the fundamental aspects of hardware and associated system software for emergent and future computing architectures for mobile, scientific, and data intensive applications. Computing systems include both mobile and fixed/virtual architectures optimized for fast communications, low power consumption, large hierarchical memory, novel and robust algorithms, high resiliency, and HPC networking. Computing science is focused on developing the understanding, tools, techniques, and methodologies to fully exploit emerging computing architectures through realization efficient parallel task algorithms and take advantage of memory hierarchies. These efforts are expected to greatly reduce the time required to restate algorithms in parallel form and correct implementation faults and bugs.

Programming Languages and processes research is focused on exploring research activities on adaptable operating system, behavioral programming languages, domain specific languages (DSL), and novel libraries. DSL's will raise the level of abstraction of the codes that programmers write, both to maintain portability across increasingly diverse hardware and to give the language implementation more scope for choosing the best route to map a program on to the most appropriate computing hardware.

Domain-specific languages (DSL) research is focused on high productivity, portability, and performance languages for Army specific applications.

(i) DSL for grid based methods focuses on improving performance, portability and productivity of finite element and finite volume methods through domain specific

languages (DSLs) and taking advantage of underlying scalable libraries and scalable algorithms.

(ii) DSL methods for graphs research is focused on developing graph applications based on a domain specific language (DSL) for graph analysis.

Processes focuses on efficiently utilizing math and engineering principles to develop reliable software.

(i) Formal methods are mathematically based techniques for the specification, development and verification of software and hardware systems. Formal methods are used to give a description of the system to be developed and guide further development activities to verify that the requirements for the system being developed have been completely and accurately specified.

(ii) Software engineering is the study and application of engineering to the design, development, and maintenance of software. However, emerging HPC systems with new architectures pose challenges in adapting software engineering practices seamlessly.

COMPUTATIONAL SCIENCES CAMPAIGN's Programming Languages and processes S&T Footprint	
S&T AREA	**POSTURE**
DSL for Grid based methods	COLLABORATE
DSL for Graphs	COLLABORATE
Formal methods	WATCH
Software engineering	COLLABORATE

Programming Environments (PE) research is focused on simplifying HPC processes associated with application analysis and software development.

Application enabling environments is focused on assisting scientific software developers, S&Es, and software users with ease of using evolving computing systems.
(i) PE for Grid and non-grid based methods research focuses on integration of high level programing models with low level programming languages to address performance challenges posed by new computing architectures.

(ii) PE Multi-physics and multi-scale methods research focuses on appropriate code coupling between different physics scales. That is, appropriate programming models are required for code coupling.

Data sharing environments is dedicated to assisting software developers and software users with ease of using evolving computing systems for data intensive applications. Disparate data from scientific simulations, experimental, sensors, and observations pose research challenges in making seamless integration with evolving computing systems.
(i) HPC Common data model and format research is focused on developing methods to effectively handle large-scale output produced by simulations. Distributed large-scale output requires fast access to manipulate the data. Appropriate standard data models and formats are needed that take advantage of access and manipulation of data, and performance on emerging computing, storage, and memory architectures.
(ii) Large-scale scientific and information sharing algorithms research is focused on new data sharing environments, algorithms and methodologies to massively reduce data intelligently during run time for simulations or at the data collection stage amenable to sharing for analytics.

COMPUTATIONAL SCIENCES CAMPAIGN's Programming Environments (PE) S&T Footprints	
S&T AREA	**POSTURE**
PE for Grid and non-grid based methods	COLLABORATE
PE Multi-physics and multi-scale methods	COLLABORATE
HPC Common data model and format	LEAD
Large-scale scientific and information sharing algorithms	COLLABORATE

Software integration is focused on using components of different application software and integrating software modules to achieve a different functionality. One approach to achieve better software, more quickly and at lower cost, we need to adopt a design process that is based on systematic software reuse. The evolution of computing infrastructure is creating new challenges, ranging from energy-aware software development to software for massively parallel and distributed systems.

Reusable software research is focused on intelligently reusing software to reduce software development time and reinventing old software.

(i) Decomposable models research is focused on large-scale system of systems software. Software architecture that facilitates decomposable models is required to explore system of system type of applications. This technology will have applicability in many other fields.

(ii) Open source community codes research is focused on leveraging software libraries and associated software tools to take advantage of emerging computing architectures.

Software portability is focused on software concepts which are transportable across multiple computing architectures and operating systems.

(i) Utility software research is focused on system software designed to analyze, configure, optimize or maintain a computer.

(ii) Automatic code generation research is focused on understanding and exploiting portable code generative programming methods.

COMPUTATIONAL SCIENCES CAMPAIGN's Software integration S&T Footprint	
S&T AREA	**POSTURE**
Decomposable Models	COLLABORATE
Open source community codes	COLLABORATE
Utility applications	WATCH
Automatic code generation	WATCH

MATERIALS RESEARCH CAMPAIGN

MISSION: Perform fundamental interdisciplinary research in materials and manufacturing science to ensure rapid and affordable development of materials, from discovery to delivery, critical to the Army of 2030.

VISION: Discovery and unparalleled innovation of devices and Materials By-Design and On-Demand across all Army domains. Understand, exploit, and demonstrate diverse material sets with exceptional quality and capabilities relevant to the Army of 2030 via advances in manufacturing science. The desired end state is to enable the Army of 2030 to succeed in distributed operations and increasingly complex environments through realization of superior materials.

MATERIALS RESEARCH CAMPAIGN PLAN

The Materials Research Campaign focuses on fundamental research to provide superior materials and devices needed to achieve lasting strategic land power dominance. Materials research cross-cuts ARL's four focused S&T campaigns by providing materials with superior properties to address emerging requirements and capabilities for all Army platforms, with emphasis on Photonics, Electronics, Energy and Power, Biological and Bio-inspired Materials, Structural Materials, High Strain and Ballistic Materials, and Manufacturing Science.

The Army of 2030 will require materials with unprecedented capabilities that can be rapidly grown or synthesized, and processed cost-effectively to enable Army platforms that are highly mobile, information reliant, lethal, and protected. The Materials Research Campaign addresses the future Army's need to rapidly respond to emerging threats and to eliminate tactical surprise – *caused by the proliferation of advanced technology by our adversaries* – by creating a materials by-design and on-demand enterprise; and a manufacturing science engine to ensure rapid progression from materials discovery to delivery, with the goal of producing materials in greatly reduced timeframes and at a fraction of the cost compared to today. Across the Materials Research campaign multi-scale models, over a range of spatial and temporal scales, are being explored to discover relevant phenomena and to enable efficient materials designs. These computational multi-scale models are closely coupled to experimental efforts to reduce uncertainty and to validate model accuracy.

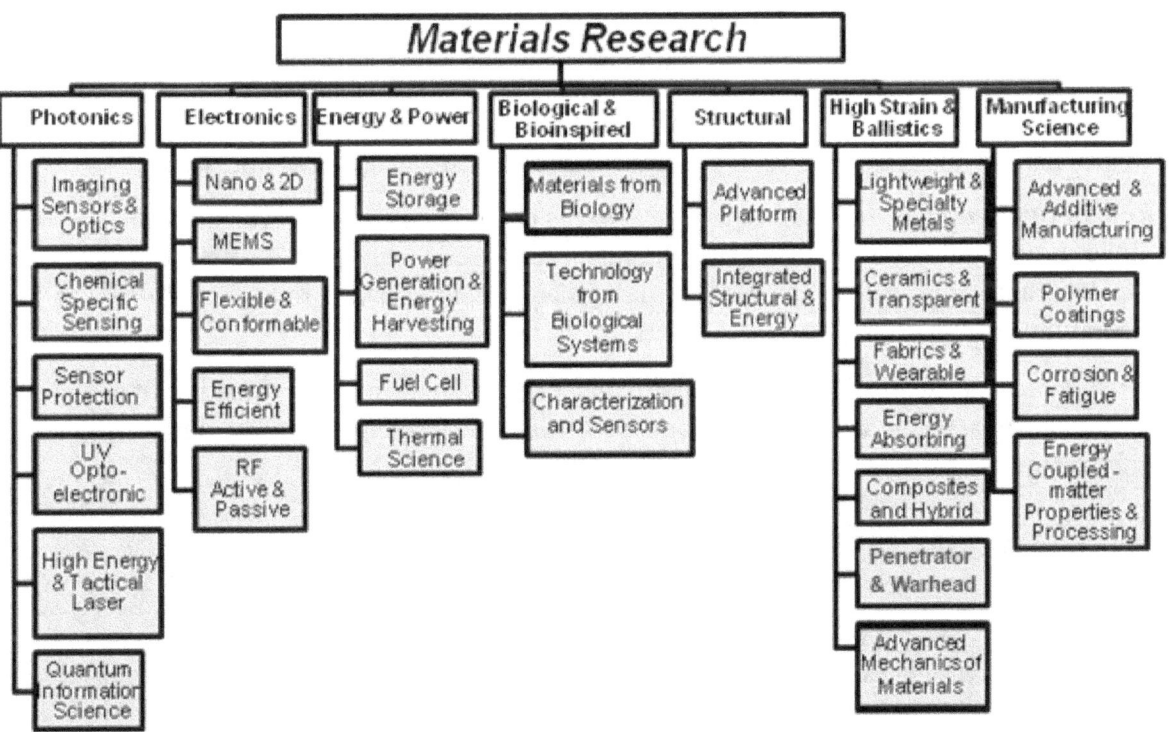

Levels 1 through 3 of the Materials Research Campaign Plan Taxonomy

PHOTONICS is focused on materials and devices for photonic sensors and sources; scalable high energy lasers; secure communications via quantum networking; and protection of sensors and human eyes against high power and short pulse laser threats.

Imaging Sensors & Optics seeks to provide increased and enhanced imaging capability to solve a diverse set of Soldier problems ranging from obscured or occluded vision, to off-axis and long-range identification, to high performance infrared imaging at higher operating temperatures with reduced size, weight, power, and cost.

Infrared Sensing Materials and Devices research includes novel electro-magnetic modeling of optical and IR devices, new material processes, and performance characterization from test pixels to focal plane arrays. Research focuses on III-V and II-VI semiconductor material growth by molecular beam epitaxy (MBE) and the design and growth of quantum well and quantum dot structures.

Transformational Optics and Devices explores research in novel optical designs to capture high resolution imagery using small size and low weight cameras. On-going work includes unique efforts in two-wavelength digital holography, structured light illumination, and non-line-of-sight ultrafast imaging.

MATERIALS RESEARCH CAMPAIGN's Imaging Sensors & Optics S&T Footprint	
S&T AREA	**POSTURE**
Infrared Sensing Materials and Devices	COLLABORATE
Transformation Optics and Devices	COLLABORATE

Chemical-specific Sensing research focuses on optical spectroscopy applied to the detection and identification of hazardous chemical, energetic, and biological materials at increased sensitivities and lower false alarm rates to improve overall sensor capability for Soldiers.

Raman Spectroscopy Techniques and Sensors is developing Coherent Raman Anti-Stokes scattering (CARS) to evaluate ultrafast laser-based techniques. Investigations are also focusing on nano-photonic structured materials for Surface-Enhanced Raman Scattering (SERS) point sensors.

Photoacoustics is investigating photothermal spectroscopy using a combination of a tunable infrared diode source and a Doppler vibrometer to determine molecular absorption information.

MATERIALS RESEARCH CAMPAIGN's Chemical-Specific sensing S&T Footprint	
S&T AREA	**POSTURE**
Raman Spectroscopy Techniques and Sensors	LEAD
Photoacoustics	COLLABORATE

Ultraviolet (UV) Optoelectronics seeks to develop new devices with enhanced material properties for UV detectors, light emitting diodes, and lasers, with applications including sensing, water purification and monitoring, threat mitigation, and communications. Nitride semiconductors materials are grown by molecular beam epitaxy (MBE) and metal organic chemical vapor deposition (MOCVD), and are characterized optically and electrically using unique ultrafast spectroscopic techniques.

Semiconductor LED & Laser UV Sources focuses on developing high power, high efficiency UV sources in the wavelength range of 205-390 nm. Research also focuses on incorporating high internal quantum efficiency nanoscale compositionally inhomogeneous AlGaN active regions on improved substrates.

UV Detectors focuses on improving out-of-band rejection and single photon detection efficiency across the UV spectral range of 220 – 400 nm. Research focuses on the growth, characterization, and design of the Nitride based photodiode detectors.

High power pulsed UV sources focuses on research of advanced materials and laser designs for efficient high peak power pulse-repetitive sources in the 240-255 nm wavelength range for hazardous materials detection systems.

MATERIALS RESEARCH CAMPAIGN's Ultra-violet (UV) Optoelectronics S&T Footprint	
S&T AREA	**POSTURE**
Semiconductor LED & Laser UV Sources	COLLABORATE
UV Detectors	LEAD
High power pulsed UV sources	LEAD

Sensor Protection explores specialty materials and devices designed to protect eyes and sensors from wavelength agile microsecond to nanosecond pulsed lasers and ultrafast lasers in multiple wavelength bands. Extensive materials characterization and modeling is used to understand nonlinear optical phenomena in specially designed and engineered organic and inorganic materials.

Active Materials focus on new materials and devices, such as electro-optical shutters, that are triggered to counter the threat of wavelength agile lasers. The current thrust is on fast time response and scalable areas

Passive Optical Materials are nonlinear materials and components that are activated by high fluence or intensity, to be placed at the optical system focal planes and only "turn on" when the system is hit with a threat laser pulse. These materials absorb, refract, scatter, or reflect ONLY the threat laser. Research is focused on improving the bandwidth of these materials and determining their utility against the emerging femtosecond threat.

MATERIALS RESEARCH CAMPAIGN's Sensor Protection S&T Footprint	
S&T AREA	**POSTURE**
Active Materials	LEAD
Passive Optical Materials	LEAD

High Energy & Tactical Lasers investigates materials for solid state lasers suitable for military applications. Research emphasizes optimized materials for device designs aimed at improving laser average and peak power, thermal management, scalability, beam quality, and efficiency to enable systems with small size, low weight, and ruggedness.

Fiber Lasers and Waveguiding Laser Devices focuses on characterization and study of materials for power scaling of resonantly pumped rare earth doped glass-based fiber lasers and Raman lasers as well as fully crystalline fiber-like laser development aiming to increase power scaling out of a single aperture by an order of magnitude.

Slab and Thin Disk Lasers focuses on the research of materials for double-faced cooled hetero-composite thin disk designs utilizing optically transparent highly thermo-conductive materials.

IR High Energy Lasers focuses on characterization and study of rare earth doped materials for high efficiency Mid-IR continuous wave and pulsed lasers and amplifiers.

MATERIALS RESEARCH CAMPAIGN's High Energy & Advanced Tactical Lasers S&T Footprint	
S&T AREA	**POSTURE**
Fiber Lasers and Waveguiding Laser Devices	COLLABORATE
Slab and Thin Disk Lasers	COLLABORATE
IR High Energy Lasers	COLLABORATE

Quantum Information Science seeks to provide ultra-precise and secure information transfer and a deeper understanding of practical quantum technologies for the Army. Research is focused on developing the knowledge to build a first-of-its-kind quantum network based on quantum memories. Emphasis is also placed on free space photon transmission and developing the network physical layer through the development and understanding of the storage and generation of photons via ion and atom traps for quantum memory, single photon detection, and controllable and scalable interconnected quantum systems.

Single Photon Sources & Detectors is the investigation of efficient generation and detection of optical photons to transfer quantum information across long distances either through optical fibers or free-space.

Quantum Control is focused on the precise manipulation of atoms, ions and photons as quantum bits for generating, retrieving, and teleporting quantum information within a quantum network.

Quantum Memory is storing quantum information by leveraging the high stability of quantum states in cold atoms to achieve long storage times.

MATERIALS RESEARCH CAMPAIGN's Quantum Information Science S&T Footprint	
S&T AREA	**POSTURE**
Single Photon Sources & Detectors	COLLABORATE
Quantum Control	COLLABORATE
Quantum Memory	COLLABORATE

ELECTRONICS is focused on specialized electronic materials and devices to achieve Army dominance over the entire electromagnetic spectrum, particularly in contested environments. The two primary thrusts of this area are Energy Efficient Electronics and Hybrid Electronics. Energy Efficient Electronics focuses on low-power-demand electronic components having increased performance capabilities; and Hybrid Electronics focuses on high performance, conformable, and flexible electronics for advanced sensors and processors.

Nano and 2D electronics research is focused on alternative electronic materials beyond silicon, and new electronic properties dominated by the interface physics of 2D materials, dissimilar materials (oxide-semiconductor, metal-semiconductor), and their quantum mechanical properties.

One Dimensional (1D) and Two Dimensional (2D) Materials exploit engineered planar crystal structures to provide distinct advantages for electronic speed and efficiency. Two dimensional materials such as molybdenum disulfide, carbon nanotubes, and graphene, are of great interest for improved electron mobility to enable lower power consumption and faster switching speeds for Soldier-borne electronics.

Integrated Quantum Structures focuses on recent advances in interface physics and engineering between dissimilar materials (oxide-semiconductor, metal-semiconductor) and their quantum mechanical properties. This includes topological insulators, van der Waal heterostructures, and novel metrology including Moiré pattern theory and Raman temperature dependence.

MATERIALS RESEARCH CAMPAIGN's Nano & 2D Electronics S&T Footprint	
S&T AREA	**POSTURE**
1D & 2D Materials	COLLABORATE
Integrated Quantum Structures	COLLABORATE

Micro-Electro-Mechanical Systems (MEMS) research explores devices for sensing, actuation, precision navigation and timing, low power digital logic, communications, and electronic warfare.

Piezoelectric MEMS is focused on applications including low power digital logic for GPS correlation, actuation for micro-robotics, and high quality factor communications, electronic warfare. Efforts focus on the maturation of LEAD zirconium titanate (PZT) and other actuator materials as well as specialized processing to increase reliability and lifetime of MEMS actuators in both digital and RF applications, and to increase energy density for unique applications. These efforts are aimed at achieving both packaged devices and heterogeneous integration of MEMs with silicon and III-V device technologies to achieve unprecedented low power and high speed solutions.

Micropower Components seeks novel constructs based on millimeter-scale power converters. MEMS components enable increased efficiency electronics components, new power distribution circuits, and enable novel power systems with greatly reduced footprint. This effort investigates novel MEMS passive structures to miniaturize and improve the power density of millimeter-scale power converters and develops integration and packaging techniques.

MATERIALS RESEARCH CAMPAIGN's MEMS S&T Footprint	
S&T AREA	**POSTURE**
Piezoelectric MEMS	LEAD
Micropower Components	LEAD

Flexible and Conformable Electronics offers the opportunity to reduce weight in systems and simplify the integration of electronics ultimately reducing Soldier burden. Focus is on unique sensor capabilities by having sensors, for example, integrated on the body when traditional electronic packaging would be unfeasible.

Flexible & Transparent Electronics is focused on novel materials and devices for the integration of silicon CMOS chips and circuit architectures in 3D additive structures to achieve flexible sensor systems for the Soldier. The materials research develops processes and understanding of integrating metals, semiconductors, dielectrics, and sensor materials in 3D additive plastic structures.

Nano-engineered Dielectrics focuses on developing polymers with higher breakdown strengths, polymer coatings with improved surface passivation, and processing approaches for manufacturing conformable electronic devices. To this end, ARL is researching dielectric polymers to develop techniques to control charge mobility by engineering molecular to nano-scale additives for capturing mobile electrons.

MATERIALS RESEARCH CAMPAIGN's Flexible & Transparent Electronics S&T Footprint	
S&T AREA	**POSTURE**
Nano-engineered Dielectrics	LEAD
Flexible & Transparent Hybrid Electronics	COLLABORATE

Energy Efficient Electronics research seeks to reduce the power consumed by analog front-end and digital back-end electronics for communication, electronic warfare, and imaging systems.

Alternative Device Technology includes heterogeneous integration of multiple device technologies for single chip RF front ends, sub-threshold silicon for low power electroencephalogram (EEG) monitoring, digital MEMs logic for long life, robust operation in extreme environments, and MEMS-based power management circuits.

RF Electronics includes material and device research for RF power amplifiers, novel circuit topologies for ultra-high efficiencies, digital processing. Low power analog and mixed signal electronics research includes state-of-the-art high frequency digital to analog converters and systems-on-chip. Also included is research address intrinsic thermal management challenges that must be met in order to realize higher efficiencies and to provide device protection in high electric field, high temperature environments.

Wide Bandgap Materials and Circuits focuses on next generation power electronic materials beyond silicon for higher reliability high voltage/current/temperature devices and circuits. Research on gallium nitride and aluminum gallium nitride materials explores growth and processing conditions to enable high quality substrates and low resistance electrical contacts. The physics of silicon carbide device and circuit failure is studied to identify limitations of current state of the art silicon carbide power electronics and develop solutions to overcome failures arising from material defects and or impurities.

MATERIALS RESEARCH CAMPAIGN's Energy Efficient Electronics S&T Footprint	
S&T AREA	**POSTURE**
Alternative Device Technology	LEAD
RF Electronics	COLLABORATE
Wide Bandgap Materials and Circuits	COLLABORATE

RF Active and Passive Materials research explores novel RF devices, circuits and metamaterials to enable future Army operations in contested environments. Research emphasis is placed on RF spectrum adaptability (cognitive RF) and the convergence of RF components to integrate communication, sensing, radar and electronic warfare (protection & attack) applications.

RF Sensing & Communications Devices is focused on cognitive RF in multiple bands for polarimetric and millimeter-wave radar, future advanced satellite communication, and short range low-power data links (60 GHz). Our efforts focus on developing millimeter-wave integrated circuits and amplifier modules at both K_a and Q-band. The convergence of communications, sensing, and radar will require additional modeling and design to implement the necessary power-optimized waveforms.

Electronic Warfare Devices is focused on high power millimeter-wave sources that must also yield greater bandwidth flexibility, enable time domain tailoring of waveforms, and LEAD to cognitive processing to adapt to the spectrum limitations of specific theaters. Focus is on developing future RF electronic warfare implementations that will eliminate the prevailing challenges of co-site and co-channel interference.

RF Metamaterials is focused on making metamaterials more suitable for practical engineering applications, particularly low profile antennas in X, K_u, and K_a bands. Research seeks to exploit greater bandwidth and isotropic properties by assembling non-periodic and randomized metamaterial structures from materials. Our goal is to obtain a greater understanding of the effects of disorder and non-periodicity on conventional metamaterial structures for additional design parameters to improve the performance and size of radiating elements.

MATERIALS RESEARCH CAMPAIGN's RF Active & Passive S& T Footprint	
S&T AREA	**POSTURE**
RF Sensing & Communications Devices	COLLABORATE
Electronic Warfare Devices	COLLABORATE
RF Metamaterials	LEAD

ENERGY AND POWER is focused on materials and devices for more efficient power generation; energy storage; energy harvesting; fuel processing; micropower; and novel alternative energy solutions at lower cost.

Energy Storage is ubiquitous in Army efforts, and improved energy storage is an enduring challenge. This materials research includes synthesis, characterization, and analysis on primary batteries, rechargeable batteries, thermal/reserve batteries, superconductor materials for superconductor magnetic energy storage, and capacitors (pulsed and continuous) for a range of applications and weapons power regimes (microwatts to megawatts).

Rechargeable and Primary Batteries is focused on new battery technologies for Army applications to improve specific energy over current lithium-ion technology as well as lower cost for storage battery technology. Improvements in electrolyte materials enable high voltage Li-ion battery operation, but more improvement and development is needed before this technology can be implemented in commercial technology. Solid electrolyte interphase is studied through in-situ characterization and multiscale modeling efforts to improve rechargeable batteries.

Munitions Batteries is developing the next generation of all-thin-film thermal batteries with faster rise, higher power, smaller volume, more flexible form-factor, and greater mechanical robustness. New chemistries or thermal management techniques are being developed to improve the performance of both the liquid reserve and thermal batteries.

Capacitors is developing high energy density dielectric and high temperature polymeric dielectric films with high breakdown strength, low dissipation factor, and moderately high dielectric constant.

Superconducting Magnetic Energy Storage focuses on Metal Organic Chemical Vapor Deposition (MOCVD) technique as means of producing superconducting thin film in high critical current density and in higher thickness. Efforts investigate Yttrium Barium Copper Oxide (YBCO) superconductor in persistent current mode and in other electronic areas and explores new composition and structure for other superconducting materials.

MATERIALS RESEARCH CAMPAIGN's Energy Storage S&T Footprint	
S&T AREA	POSTURE
Rechargeable and Primary Batteries	LEAD
Munitions Batteries	LEAD
Capacitors	COLLABORATE
Superconducting Magnetic Energy Storage	COLLABORATE

Power Generation & Energy Harvesting is essential for the sustainment of all Army operations. This research seeks to improve the conversion efficiency of generation and harvesting technology, and bring novel approaches to energy harvesting to usable levels.

Thermal Energy Conversion focuses primarily on improving thermophotovoltaic and thermoelectric energy conversion materials and devices for portable power and sensor platform power generation, waste-heat recovery, and thermal energy harvesting. Thermoelectric efforts focus on improving the conversion efficiency of multi-stage thermoelectric materials and devices while addressing the parasitic aspects of the device packaging. Thermophotovoltaic efforts focus on developing low bandgap (0.5 eV – 0.6 eV) photovoltaic cells using molecular beam epitaxy (MBE) growth techniques, high temperature thermally stable optical filters, and integration with combustion-based heat sources from the Fuel Flexible Combustion-based Power Sources S&T sub area.

Fuel Flexible Combustion-based Power Sources focuses on identification and synthesis of alloyed catalyst materials that enable higher conversion, are more durable to carbon formation, have improved sulfur tolerance, and are cost effective compared to platinum for the combustion of JP-8 and use in portable power devices. This effort also focuses on materials, components and integration for compact vaporization and combustion of liquid fuels and alternative sources for efficient thermal sources to develop power sources using energy conversion from the Thermal Energy Conversion S&T sub area.

Ultra-energetic Radionuclides focuses on identification of radio-isotope sources best suited for sensor and board-level power supply applications and investigating wide-bandgap materials (SiC, GaN, and diamond) for radiation tolerance, conversion efficiency and optimal device design matched to keV level β-semiconductor interaction. Indirect energy conversion is also being investigated offering short-term solutions for device evaluation.

Alternative Routes to Fuel enables energy self-sufficiency to reduce the logistics footprint and the need to resupply energy sources. The area focuses on exploiting emerging materials, structures and processes such as bandgap and structurally engineered materials designed to break C-C and H-O-H bonds; CO_2 electroreduction at room temperature; plasmonic and metamaterial structures for catalysis and energy transduction; and related constructs for device and energy integration.

Energy Harvesting places emphasis on multimodal energy harvesting and leverages the MEMS Micropower Components S&T sub area to allow capture of radiant energy (light, vibration, temperature) in discrete packages capable of storing and supplying energy to a Soldier or sensor. Efficient lightweight, low cost solar photovoltaic devices are explored focusing on omnidirectional light trapping structures on III-V photovoltaic systesm.

MATERIALS RESEARCH CAMPAIGN's Power Generation & Energy Harvesting S&T Footprint	
S&T AREA	**POSTURE**
Thermal Energy Conversion	COLLABORATE
Fuel Flexible Micro/Meso-scale Combustion Materials and Devices	LEAD
Alternative Routes to Fuel	LEAD
Ultra-energetic Radionuclides	LEAD
Energy Harvesting	COLLABORATE

Fuel Cell research focuses on augmenting or replacing battery power with high energy density, fuel-flexible power sources to lighten the load for the Soldiers and Army platforms, and to reduce the logistics.

Fuel Cells is focused on miniaturizing and reducing the cost of liquid fueled, high energy density Solider wearable and portable fuel cell power sources through the development of Alkaline and Hybrid fuel cells and developing new electrolytes, membranes, and catalysts.

JP-8 Fuel Reformation and Conditioning focuses on the development of high capacity and regenerable sulfur sorbents, and low cost, highly selective hydrogen separation membranes for the processing of logistics fuel for use in larger (>100 watts) high-efficiency fuel cell power sources.

MATERIALS RESEARCH CAMPAIGN's Fuel Cell S&T Footprint	
S&T AREA	**POSTURE**
Fuel Cells	LEAD
JP-8 Fuel Reformation and Conditioning	COLLABORATE

Thermal Science enables increased reliability and improved size, weight of power electronics, energy conversion technologies, and environmental control units. This research focuses on thermal transport and control materials and techniques including: electronics cooling, heat reclamation, integrated device packaging and cooling, micro channel cooling, phase change transient thermal management, two-phase liquid heat sinks, condensation and heat rejection enhancement, and semiconductor device-level thermal improvement.

Electronics Packaging and Thermal Interfaces focuses on measurements and reduction of interfacial resistance at the package level, the development of heat rejection techniques via condensation and radiation, and 3D packaging with integrated cooling to significantly reduce package inductance while maintaining adequate electronics cooling.

Two-Phase Heat Transfer focuses on improved performance by increasing the heat transfer coefficient, reducing pumping power and allowing for better temperature uniformity. Development of advanced heat sink technology for power electronics focuses on two-phase flow in inner grooved tubes to transition to a higher heat transfer flow regime. Research is also focused on the integration of solid-liquid phase change material (PCM) into heat sinks for device peak temperature reduction.

MATERIALS RESEARCH CAMPAIGN's Thermal Science S&T Footprint	
S&T AREA	**POSTURE**
Advanced Electronics Packaging and Thermal Interfaces	LEAD
Two-Phase Heat Transfer	LEAD

BIOLOGICAL AND BIO-INSPIRED is focused on discovery and manufacture of new materials from biology, development of novel biotechnologies from biomaterials, and characterization of biomaterials through novel and classical approaches. Materials from biology are combined with inorganic materials or processes to design devices for sensing and characterization of chemical and biological materials, generate power, engineer complex protection materials with designs inspired by nature, and for multi-functional purposes.

Materials from Biology can enable advancements in protective materials, therapeutics, responsive materials, sensor technology, manufacturing, renewable materials, and intelligence. By determining the evolutionary solutions and fundamental design criteria or rules that nature follows, we can synthesize complex materials with designed protection, sensor, and multi-functional properties, or harness biological organisms to produce them.

Hard and Soft Tissue Simulants research goals are to understand factors that control the strain and strain rate dependent mechanical response of soft synthetic polymers; develop multiscale computational and experimental characterization tools to quantify the structure and mechanical response of soft polymers and biotissues; to design synthetic polymers that mimic rate dependent response of human body tissue (both soft tissues and bone) for head, torso, and extremity forms that will be exploited in testing protocols for protective equipment; and to develop environmentally stable and transparent synthetic materials as replacement candidates for ballistic gelatin and ballistic clay. The materials include synthetic gels for mimics of soft biological tissues and rigid polymers for mimics of skull.

Bio-Mimetic Materials seeks to develop understanding of the evolutionary solutions created by nature, to understand the fundamental design rules, create similar structures using synthetic materials, and evaluate sensing approaches applied to relevant targets. Bio-inspired metal-ligand cross-linking strategies for polymer reinforcement are currently under investigation, and hierarchically structured composites and networks are being explored to optimize trade-offs between toughness and yield strength. The Army is uniquely concerned with material and device performance under extreme conditions, including temperature and humidity extremes and high-rate events.

Biosynthetic Materials research is a sub-discipline of Synthetic Biology and focuses on engineering biology and biotechnology for the production of materials. There is not yet a significant industrial driver for this area. However, it is anticipated that specific applications could include production of made-to-order polysaccharides and commodity chemicals to reduce the logistical burden. Current research at the experimentation and modeling level is aimed at developing the bioengineering tools for control of organism biosynthesis, and is coordinated with the Technologies from Biological Systems S&T sub area.

Bio/Non-Bio Interface Materials focuses on developing an understanding and approaches to interface biological and non-biological materials for multi-scalar systems. Understanding the phenomena that govern biocompatibility will aid in the development of biosensor systems, which are a current focus, but could be extended to bioelectronics, lithographic techniques for advanced materials synthesis, and prosthetics. Key areas include the use of a microbial library to explore peptide-based binding motifs to target specific substrate adhesive interactions and synthetic adhesives employing biologically-inspired strategies for improving adhesive interactions.

Green Material and Processes focuses on computational and experimental methods to investigate the design, preparation, and characterization of polymers derived from renewable sources. The research investigates computational methods to predict properties of bio-derived polymers.

Biopolymer Adhesives is harnessing the chemical variability found in naturally occurring adhesive proteins and translating them into commercial adhesives, accomplished through a concerted modeling and synthetic effort and leveraging emerging materials science. The program develops a fundamental understanding regarding the drivers of adhesion under a variety of loading conditions and strain rates, and improves substrate-adhesive interactions to improve performance under a range of temperature and humidity extremes.

MATERIALS RESEARCH CAMPAIGN's Materials from Biology S&T Footprint	
S&T AREA	POSTURE
Hard and Soft Tissue Simulants	LEAD
Bio-Mimetic Materials	COLLABORATE
Biosynthetic Materials	COLLABORATE
Bio/Non-Bio Interfaces	COLLABORATE
Green Material and Processes	COLLABORATE
Biopolymer Adhesives	COLLABORATE

Technologies from Biological Systems research is focused on Army challenges in power and energy, waste remediation, lightweight systems, and energy absorption. Emphasis is placed on the complex relationships existing within and between levels of biological organization, living organisms, and their environment. Genomics, Transcriptomics, Proteomics, and Metabolomics are emerging disciplines at ARL that require an adaptable S&T strategy for Army bioscience needs. Hybrid technologies that incorporate biological organisms will improve situational awareness, as well as sustainability and logistics through alternative energy sources, waste mitigation, water management, and resource conservation.

Systems Biology, Synthetic Biology, and Bioinformatics research aims at discovering the natural principles that underlie organism metabolism, exploiting the large data sets that result, and using the discovered principles to engineer organisms for desired tasks for logistics reduction. Tools are being developed to understand and use the large data sets resulting from the generation and collection of vast amounts of data from genomics, transcriptomics, proteomics, and metabolomics. Work presently focuses on microbial systems that could be capable of converting waste feedstocks into commodity chemicals and is coordinated with the Materials from Biology S&T sub area. This technology area will be critical to the Army's requirements of improved Soldier performance, sustainability, and increased maneuverability.

In-Situ and Integrative Biology research enables engineering robust, stable systems for biological processes at useful scales in a safe manner. Current engineered systems tend to be fragile; losing their engineered characteristics over time or when exposed to other organisms. Successful research would enhance situational awareness, sustainability and soldier performance.

Bio Energy is focused on how biology produces energy for its own consumption as well as how that energy could be harnessed for Army applications. This research extends beyond biofuels production to metabolic processes for the production of commodity chemicals, photosynthetic technologies, bio- and bio-hybrid fuel cells as well as an emphasis on waste mitigation and waste-to-energy.

MATERIALS RESEARCH CAMPAIGN's Technologies from Biological Systems S&T Footprint	
S&T AREA	**POSTURE**
Systems Biology, Synthetic Biology and Bioinformatics	COLLABORATE
In-Situ and Integrative Biology	COLLABORATE
Bio Energy	COLLABORATE

Characterization and Sensors includes two areas. The first area involves experimentation and modeling for the characterization of biomaterials in support of the Biological and Bio-Inspired technical focus area and that can feed into other areas including bio-inspired systems and human science research. The second area involves research that informs the development and assessment of sensors and characterization devices for environmental chemical and biological materials. Research in these two areas can LEAD to new capabilities in areas including Soldier protection, performance optimization, sustainment, sensing and monitoring, situational awareness, and forensic capabilities for military intelligence.

Environmental Biological Materials is focused on a baseline understanding of the naturally occurring biological constituents within the Army's operating environment to inform the development and assessment of biological sensors as well as the forensic capabilities of military intelligence, and includes understanding atmospheric and microenvironmental effects on biologicals, and techniques for characterizing biologicals.

Biometrics, Bio-imaging, and Monitoring research is directed at technologies with a biological or bio-inspired component for sensing bio materials (e.g., biomolecules, cells, organisms) and chemical materials, as well as non-biological technologies for sensing biological materials. Examples include development of spectroscopic methods and related algorithms for sensing microbes, biological-based methods for sensing biochemicals in support wearable technologies, and imaging techniques along with their computational algorithms to assess vital parameters of the body at range.

Characterization of Biomaterials focuses on multi-scale experimentation and modeling to characterize molecular, biochemical, and cellular mechanisms to feed into computational biology efforts in support of the Biological and Bio-inspired technical focus area as well as other technical focus areas. This level of understanding is required, for example, to engineer systems of microbes to carry out purposes useful for the Soldier, such as waste-to-energy conversion. Furthermore, by examining interactions between the various scales, one can exploit atomic, cellular, or biochemical scale advancements to improve Soldier performance, sustainability, and maneuverability under Army-unique conditions.

Biomechanics studies how mechanical forces shape the structure and function of biological systems and materials. From the micro to macro scale, research into human kinematics, tissue deformation, cellular behavior and physiologic functions have great potential to improve combat effectiveness and warfighter performance. Current applications include novel armor design, robotics technology and the enhancement of weapon lethality.

MATERIALS RESEARCH CAMPAIGN's Characterization and Sensors S&T Footprint	
S&T AREA	POSTURE
Environmental Biologicals	LEAD
Biometrics, Bio-imaging, and Monitoring	LEAD
Characterization of Bio Materials	COLLABORATE
Biomechanics	COLLABORATE

STRUCTURAL MATERIALS is focused on novel and specialized materials to enhance the structural efficiency and systems performance of advanced platform structures while maintaining the same or greater levels of protection compared to today's platforms.

Advanced Platform Structures includes investigations into polymeric materials for use as adhesives. Applications include microfluidic appliqués with adaptive optical and electromagnetic properties. Goals of this research include characterization of failure modes at high rates and altering and control of these modes through novel surface preparation.

Adaptive Microfluidic Surface Appliqués have the potential to create surfaces with adaptive optical and thermal properties. Focus is on developing the microfluidic design and fabrication techniques for robust and repeatable operation.

Nanoengineered Polymers will develop novel processing strategies to control nano-to-micro scale structure in polymers, which will in turn enable tunable mechanical response across a broad range of strain rates. Systematic control over inclusion size, distribution, shape, and orientation will permit unprecedented correlation of microstructure with mechanical and strain rate response. The experimental component is combined with advanced multi-scale computational modeling of polymer structure and mechanical response to both validate computational tools and allow for predictive description of mechanical characteristics.

Hybrid 3D Composites research focuses on reinforcement and strengthening of composite materials in the thickest direction as a solution to composite armor to meet protection requirements with reduced weight and cost. Full 3D weaving of the composite reinforcement material is being investigated and includes new modeling tools, lower cost and low damage methods and the use of compliant interlayers to reduce composite delamination.

MATERIALS RESEARCH CAMPAIGN's Advanced Platform Structures S&T Footprint	
S&T AREA	POSTURE
Adaptive Microfluidic Surface Appliqués	LEAD
Nanoengineered Polymers	COLLABORATE
Hybrid 3D Composite Armor	COLLABORATE

Integrated Structural & Energy Materials takes advantage of multifunctional materials concepts where the multifunctionality is derived from a "structure-plus" concept. Efforts in this area focus on introducing energy storage capability into structural materials. Current capability is limited by the structural dielectric and the need to balance power storage with structural integrity.

Multifunctional Nanocomposite Dielectrics materials achieve system-level mass and volume savings by combining several functions (energy storage and ballistic protection) into a single material. This research seeks to invent multifunctional, structural composite capacitors with an unprecedented combination of mechanical and electrical properties, incorporating high performance ballistic film dielectrics as well as graphene based electrodes. Furthermore, increases in energy density will be pursued through fundamental studies on the origin and mechanism for breakdown in a composite dielectric.

Multifunctional Materials is developing structural batteries and supercapacitors that can both store electrical energy and carry mechanical loads. The systems consist of multifunctional cathode, anode, and electrolyte materials that serve both structural and electrochemical functions.

MATERIALS RESEARCH CAMPAIGN's Integrated Structural & Energy S&T Footprint	
S&T AREA	**POSTURE**
Multifunctional Nanocomposite Dielectrics	LEAD
Multifunctional Structural Materials	COLLABORATE

HIGH STRAIN RATE AND BALLISTIC MATERIALS is focused on novel and specialized materials to enhance the performance and efficiency of Army weapons and protection systems including lightweight, extreme performance materials; novel energetic materials; and energy absorbing materials.

Lightweight & Specialty Metals researches the use of lightweight metals for application to a variety of platforms including the reduction of Soldier equipment and vehicle platforms. Other materials investigations include tungsten carbide composition and process development. The desired tungsten carbide compositions contain no cobalt and studies explore densification methods.

Processing Nano-scale Metallics research focuses on precise chemical control to achieve and maintain specific grain size at elevated temperatures to aid in the bulk consolidation of nanocrystalline metals. Research is focused on the development of a robust thermodynamic approach to stabilizing nanocrystalline grain size which is applicable to numerous metal systems, including bulk applications for lightweight alloys used in armor as well as alloys for lethality, and advanced coating technologies.

Nanocrystalline Tungsten Alloys research focuses on development of novel tungsten alloys and microstructures to improve strength, ductility and high rate deformation properties of tungsten alloys. Material improvements will serve to improve the reliability, sustainability and lethality of various kinetic energy munitions technologies.

Optimized Tungsten Carbide focuses on identifying the tungsten carbide microstructure and properties as well as the projectile nose geometry required to maintain rigid body penetration over a range of impact obliquities.

Integrated Processing for Enhanced Durability is focused on design to identify the fundamental scientific mechanisms and processing, characterization, and computational methods that will result in the development of ultra-high strength Mg alloys.

Magnesium is focused on providing a well-grounded basis for the utilization of Mg- and Mg-based alloys in an Army relevant application, wherein the advantageous aspects are fully maximized, and the disadvantages are mitigated.

Aluminum for Vehicle Protection is focused on developing and maturing new metallic materials and encapsulation processing techniques, for kinetic energy (KE) armors which are affordable and sufficiently mature. Also included is research to determine the effectiveness of the various strengthening mechanisms in Al alloys - when subjected to dynamic loading and understand their role in ballistic performance. Research seeks to investigate readily formable aluminum alloys amenable to monolithic formed underbodies that achieve peak strength, elongation, and toughness after forming and transition to the aluminum industry.

Gun Barrel Improvement aims to extend the service life of gun barrels via increased temperature resistance and improved cooling through novel designs and materials. Potential solutions include the Gun Liner Emplacement by Elastomeric Material (GLEEM) process and explosive bonding incorporating Ta10W and hammer forged BioDur which will enhance life while eliminating hexavalent chrome use in liners.

MATERIALS RESEARCH CAMPAIGN's Lightweight & Specialty Metals S&T Footprint	
S&T AREA	**POSTURE**
Ultrafine Grain Nanocrystalline and Amorphous Tungsten Alloys	LEAD
Integrated Processing for Enhanced Durability & Nano-scale Metallics	LEAD
Optimized Tungsten Carbide	LEAD
Study of Fundamental Penetration Phenomena	LEAD
Magnesium	COLLABORATE
Aluminum for vehicle protection	COLLABORATE
Gun Barrel Improvement	COLLABORATE

Ceramics and Transparent research examines lightweight boron-based compositions and novel transparent materials for Soldier and platform protection. Boron carbide and alternative compositions of B_6O and AlB_{12} offer lightweight and high hardness. Research in this area focuses on processing techniques and methods by which the ceramic materials fail. Research in transparent materials includes materials based on polymers reinforced with naturally derived nanocrystalline cellulose and effects of glass composition on ballistic resistance.

Boron-based Ceramics research is focused on developing processes which enable the synthesis of boron-icosahedral based monolithic ceramics and ceramic composites with enhanced fracture resistance and quasi-plasticity through the creation of doped grain boundary films, amorphous or crystalline, oxide or nonoxide, and nanoscale or submicron. Focus is on incorporating doped grain boundary films in boron carbide and boron suboxide.

Ceramics for Protection encompasses the nondestructive characterization and ballistic evaluation of silicon carbide and other candidate ceramic formulations. Tiles comprised of these materials will have been formed using conventional and developmental densification methods in order to reduce costs and improve ballistic C21 performance. Statistics is employed to correlate ballistic performance to the processing history with the goal of identifying improved microstructures.

Transparent Polymer-Polymer Composites research goal is to develop tough, transparent polymer-polymer composites for Soldier and vehicle protection. While composites have provided significant advances in performance for opaque armor applications, they are not transparent because the many interfaces in these materials scatter and refract light. In this work we seek to demonstrate transparent composites by incorporating polymer ribbon reinforcement into a refractive-index-matched matrix.

Inelastic Deformation Mechanisms in SiC research strives to identify the inelastic deformation ("bulk plasticity") mechanisms present in armor ceramics by bridging the strain scale. The role of each mechanism with respect to strain rate will be determined. An understanding of inelastic deformation mechanisms and the role they play in a materials response to a ballistic impact event can be transitioned to the materials processing and development community to develop armor ceramics with improved ballistic performance.

Multiscale Modeling of AlON research goal is to develop a concurrent multiscale computational code to predict the performance and optimize the design of brittle transparent ceramic materials not yet synthesized. A specific computational challenge is to model the interplay between transgranular and intergranular fracture deformation mechanisms in anisotropic polycrystalline transparent materials using ARL's peridynamics code.

Nanocellulose Transparent Composites research focuses on utilizing bioderived cellulose nanocrystals to improve modulus and fracture toughness of transparent polymers. The effort focuses on understanding and control over the hierarchical nanoarchitectures and their surface interactions towards targeted properties. The ultimate objective is to obviate delamination problems by replacing transparent laminates with reinforced monoliths exhibiting superior performance.

MATERIALS RESEARCH CAMPAIGN's Ceramic & Transparent S&T Footprint	
S&T AREA	POSTURE
Boron-based Ceramics	LEAD
Ceramics for Protection	LEAD
Transparent Polymer-Polymer Composites	LEAD
Inelastic Deformation Mechanisms in SiC	LEAD
Electromagnetic Ceramic Confinement	LEAD
Multiscale Modeling of AlON	LEAD
Nanocellulose Transparent Composites	COLLABORATE

Fabrics and Wearable research explores high-rate penetration resistance properties of monolithic and hybrid fabrics for unprecedented strength and stiffness. Computational capabilities explore nanoscale structure-property relationships, atomistic level constitutive properties, and relationships to bridge from single fiber level to yarn level properties. Laser-based chemical vapor deposition (CVD) techniques explore rapid graphene growth.

3D Woven Fabric demonstrates new capabilities by incorporating fiber level properties into simulations which include high speed penetration of multi-layer 3D fabrics with enhanced ballistic resistant capacity.

Multiscale Response of Fibers and Fabrics is focused on developing a fabric ballistic modeling tool that will enable a true fabric-by-design capability for rapid development of advanced soft body protection. A numerical tool using multi-scale approach is being developed to accurately predict fabric ballistic behavior that will enable optimal ballistic fabric design. A molecular dynamic modeling tool and novel small scale mechanics techniques is being developed to link molecular level defects and morphology to mesoscale single fiber response. Capabilities are also being developed to bridge from the single filament scale to the yarn level/macroscale will also be established.

Knit Architecture for Comfort and Protection is focused on continuous filament knitted aramids (CFKA) materials to provide a unique combination of stretchability and ballistic protection, and could be used to provide extremity protection without significant compromise in wearer comfort.

Degradation Effects of Ballistic Fibers research focuses on the effect of environmental mechanisms such as UV, temperature, and humidity on the morphology stiffness and strength found in ballistic fibers. Focus is on structure/property relationships of para-aramids and ultrahigh molecular weight polyethylene.

Improved Models for Soft Body Armor is focused on enhancing existing modeling code via ballistic simulations of 2D fabric (up to 30 layers) with multiple materials. A highly computational hybrid mesh will be developed to reduce the computation time. The accuracy of using the hybrid mesh on computing ballistic limits of multi-layer fabrics will be validated by comparing the predicted results with experimental data.

Membrane Materials seeks to create new membranes that can be used in CB-protective garments as a water vapor transport layer. Key characteristics include water vapor transport and mechanical toughness.

MATERIALS RESEARCH CAMPAIGN's Fabrics and Wearable S&T Footprint	
S&T AREA	**POSTURE**
3D Woven Fabric	LEAD
Multiscale Response of Fibers and Fabrics	LEAD
Knit Architecture for Comfort and Protection	LEAD
Degradation Effects of Ballistic Fibers	COLLABORATE
Improved Models for Soft Body Armor	COLLABORATE
Membrane Materials	COLLABORATE

Energy Absorber research focuses on the behavior of polymer networks in mechanical environments for vehicle protection. The goals are to develop an understanding of the chemical, physical, and structural factors that influence the strain rate dependent mechanical response of glassy polymer networks (epoxies) and seek new network designs with enhanced rate dependent properties.

Ion-containing Polymers is developing new ion-containing polymers for use as solid polyelectrolytes in fuel cells. Key areas of research include designing continuous charge transport pathways and improving the mechanical properties of the resulting materials. This program also includes work on materials that include easily tailored structure and properties through the use of chemical moieties for metal ion-ligand bonds.

Behavior of Polymer Networks research goals are to understand the chemical, physical, and structural factors that control the strain rate dependent mechanical response of glassy polymer networks; and to design new networks with enhanced rate dependent energy dissipation. The research focuses on the high strain rate regime which is essentially unexplored for these polymers.

Energy Absorbing Materials for Underbody Blast Mitigation is working on lightweight energy absorbing metallic, composite and hybrid materials for vehicle structure (exterior and interior) that can provide substantial improvement on crew protection subjected to blast and ballistic threats. It includes energy absorption material for vehicle structure, vehicle flooring and seating systems.

Energy Dissipating Materials - Foams and Honeycombs for Helmet Application is developing new materials engineered to maximize energy absorption within the available space between helmet shell and head to attenuate impulsive loading due to blunt impact. The research focuses on creating padding systems based on foams and composites that dissipate energy to limit head acceleration to below the injury tolerance limit.

Auxetic Materials are a sub-set of meta-materials which have been identified as a potential disruptive technology. An auxetic material that expands laterally as it is stretched has potential for use in protection applications because significant energy is absorbed while being lightweight. The program seeks to improve the fundamental understanding of inherently auxetic molecules for protection.

MATERIALS RESEARCH CAMPAIGN's Energy Absorber S&T Footprint	
S&T AREA	**POSTURE**
Ion-containing Polymers	LEAD
Behavior of Polymer Networks	LEAD
Energy Absorbing Materials for Underbody Blast Mitigation	LEAD
Energy Dissipating Materials - Foams and Honeycombs for Helmet Application	LEAD
Concurrent Multi-mechanism Deformation of Condensed Matter	COLLABORATE
Energy Absorbing Imaging and Velocimetry	COLLABORATE
Auxetic Materials	WATCH

Composites and Hybrid identifies high rate mechanisms, materials, processes, and concepts required to enable quantifiable improvement in soldier and vehicle protection. The effort applies model and tool suite development for computational solutions, composite material and architecture lay-ups, improved processing to circumvent void formation in processed materials, and the incorporation of multi-scale materials integration. Research also examines the process-property-performance relationships associated with ultrahigh molecular weight polyethylene (UHMWPE) composites. Multi-physics models are being developed to predict the influence of processing on the properties of the fiber tow/matrix/interface constituents.

Process and Modeling UHMWPE effort seeks to gain a fundamental understanding of the complex processing-property-performance relationships associated with highly ballistic efficient materials. This research will guide the development of processing and characterization strategies for enhanced ballistic performance and provide multi-scale constitutive models for more accurate hydrocode simulations - ultimately improving UHMWPE composite armors for the individual warfighter and protective systems to support future Army platforms.

Novel Synthesis Routes for Graphene is developing novel synthesis routes via unconventional thermal processing for dramatic increases in production rates during graphene growth. Focus is on experiments and characterization of resulting graphene structures.

Composites and Adhesives Development seeks to understand complex material property relationships necessary to field optimal protection schemes. Emphasis is on accelerating development to meet Army bonding requirements for bonded composites in short time-frames.

Advanced Materials and Processes for Head Protection goal is to identify the high-rate mechanisms, materials, processes, and concepts required for enabling quantifiable improvement in key aspects of Soldier-borne head protection. This includes a ballistic helmet capable of defeating theater-relevant small arms threats as well as new insight and approaches to mitigating the shock and adverse impulses associated with impact.

Durable Hybrid Composites research seeks to improve the durability and damage tolerance of thick composites for Army structural/armor applications using interlaminar enhancement techniques such as compliant interlayers and needling technologies. Focus is on lightweight composites subjected to Army relevant load spectrums (multiple impact, high energy impact, and high to low cycle fatigue) to meet the needs of current and future Army platforms and structures.

Composite Models research is focused on developing improved multi-scale composite models for implementation into our broad-based materials-by-design approach to advance state-of-the-art materials. This research is developing the complex scale-bridging techniques that link molecular length scales up to the full-scale structure, with particular emphasis on the behavior of materials under extreme dynamic environments. Focus is on enabling the design of lighter weight, more advanced materials and systems to support the individual warfighter and future Army platforms.

MATERIALS RESEARCH CAMPAIGN's Composite & Hybrid S&T Footprint	
S&T AREA	**POSTURE**
Process and Modeling UHMWPE	LEAD
Microstructured Materials for Armor	LEAD
Carbon Nanotube Coated Fibers	LEAD
Novel Synthesis Routes for Graphene	LEAD
Composites and Adhesives Development	COLLABORATE
Advanced Materials and Processes for Head Protection	COLLABORATE
Processing and Fabrication Effects	COLLABORATE
Durable Hybrid Composites	COLLABORATE
Composite Models	COLLABORATE

Penetrator and Warhead Materials research investigates the use of nanocrystalline tungsten materials for the replacement of depleted uranium (DU). Research also investigates the replacement of conventional tracers with a phosphorescent material to provide one-way luminescence, and developing a material that charges in the gun barrel, emits at the desired wavelength, and emits for the required length of time.

Enhanced Lethality Warhead Mechanism RP3 UFG Liners for Warheads research seeks to develop bulk, stable nanocrystalline materials with tailored properties for Future ballistic applications such as shaped charge liners and explosively formed penetrators (EFPs). Focus is on the development and exploitation of new nanocrystalline composite metallic systems, innovative processing and characterization methodologies, and integration of computational materials science and engineering tools and frameworks.

Enabling Technology for KE RP2 Replacement DU focuses on the development of processing methods to improve strength, ductility and high rate deformation properties of tungsten alloys. Material improvements will serve to improve the reliability, sustainability and lethality of various kinetic energy munitions technologies.

One Way Luminescence (Daylight Tracer) research addresses development of non-combustible tracer technology to replace current combustible tracers, which lose mass during flight causing trajectory mismatch and reducing overall lethality. Research will replace combustible materials with a light emitting coating that can be applied to any bullet to transform it into a day tracer projectile that retains mass and trace accuracy. Low observable tracer coating will also have a reduced viewing angle that can be seen only by shooter, eliminating two-way visibility of combustible tracers that allow the target to locate shooter and return fire.

Kinetic Energy Penetrators investigates microstructural engineering to achieve shear localization behavior in highly dense tungsten-based materials for replacement of depleted uranium (DU) penetrators to reduce toxicity and environmental impact. This research will utilize key areas of materials research to produce ultra-fine grained, nanocrystalline and amorphous materials by using severe plastic deformation, bottom-up powder metallurgy and alloying approaches.

MATERIALS RESEARCH CAMPAIGN's Penetrator and Warhead S&T Footprint	
S&T AREA	**POSTURE**
Enhanced Lethality Warhead Mechanism RP3 UFG Liners for Warheads	LEAD
Enabling Technology for KE RP2 Replacement DU	COLLABORATE
One Way Luminescence (Daylight Tracer)	COLLABORATE
Kinetic Energy Penetrators	COLLABORATE

Advanced Mechanics of Materials seeks to develop improved understanding of impact dynamics for applications in lethality and protection. This effort focuses on understanding the response of materials and structures subjected to intense short-duration loading under conditions over a wide range of velocity impacts.

MATERIALS RESEARCH CAMPAIGN's Advanced Mechanics S&T Footprint	
S&T AREA	**POSTURE**
Advanced Mechanics of Materials	LEAD

MANUFACTURING SCIENCE is focused on discovery, innovation, and maturation of manufacturing innovations to facilitate agile, adaptive, mobile processing and manufacturing capabilities to enable superior performance and implementation of cost reduction methodologies. Sustainability is focused on understanding material properties and degradation mechanisms to improve durability of Army systems in extreme environments.

Advanced and Additive Manufacturing seeks to explore the manufacturing tools necessary to field novel materials technologies and new production methods to reduce costs for Army systems.

Indigenous Materials research goal is to develop processing science to enable adaptive, mobile manufacturing of indigenous materials. Not only will indigenous materials be the focus of this research, but also recycled and reclaimed materials typically found in an operational environment, in an effort to create useful products for the warfighter.

Adhesive Processing research is focused on defining consistent long-term best practices and standards to meet the wide breadth of critical Army bonding requirements.

Guidance in this area required by PM's faced with immediate urgency for fielded bonded solutions, which often results on long-term durability and sustainability issues at increased repair/replacement costs.

Advanced Manufacturing focuses on the refinement of emerging manufacturing methods such as field-assisted sintering technology (FAST), cold spray deposition of materials, and investigating the feasibility of using indigenous materials to manufacture component parts. Long term goals are to fully link virtual manufacturing and computational materials by design with simulation and engineering design tools.

Additive Manufacturing is investigating the use of cold spray processing as an additive manufacturing tool. This research investigates the use of hybrid concepts to improve additive build rates while maintain resolution. The hybrid concepts achieves bulk part formation with high rate cold spray deposition while fine detail is added using slower laser forming techniques. The technical challenge lies in combining these vastly different additive processes.

Field Assisted Manufacturing research focuses on developing revolutionary primary and secondary manufacturing processes that are direct consequences of the combined intrinsic mechanisms in metastable thermodynamics activated by the extrinsic applied fields. The research also focuses on establishing unconventional manufacturing innovations to precisely control nonequilibrium multiphase/component kinetics independently and selectively by manipulating discrete or hybridized fields applied at the subsystem or system manufacturing levels to expand manufacturability and scalability well beyond the current state of the art.

Process Simulation/Virtual Manufacturing research is focused on developing an integrated computational materials engineering (ICME) framework which links the effects of primary and secondary processing to the microstructure and properties of materials through the lifecycle of a manufactured component. Advanced numerical modeling tools are developed and implemented at multiple length scales to simulate processing, microstructural evolution, microstructure specific mechanical properties, and final structural performance based on individualized processing history of the component(s) in order to optimize design and manufacturability of Army systems with enhanced capability and performance.

Joining, Machining, and Assembly research focuses on the welding and joining of advanced and dissimilar material combinations to achieve enhanced properties and superior performance. The focus is on lightweight materials that can perform in extreme environments and applications. This is addressed by controlling welding and joining parameters to optimize final microstructures.

Design for Materials and Manufacturing research focuses on incorporating integrated computational materials engineering (ICME) and design for manufacturing principles concurrently. This research is developing tools to provide optimized design using advanced materials with concurrent design of the manufacturing process.

MATERIALS RESEARCH CAMPAIGN's Advanced & Additive Manufacturing S&T Footprint	
S&T AREA	**POSTURE**
Indigenous Materials	LEAD
Adhesive Processing	LEAD
Advanced Manufacturing	COLLABORATE
Additive Manufacturing	COLLABORATE
Field Assisted Manufacturing	COLLABORATE
Process Simulation/Virtual Manufacturing	COLLABORATE
Joining, Machining and Assembly	COLLABORATE
Design for Materials and Manufacturing	COLLABORATE

Polymer Coatings research focuses on the development of high performance, sustainable chemical agent resistant coatings (CARC), including non-isocyanate chemistries, which exceed current coating systems. Full structure-property relationships that relate gloss, adhesion, mar resistance, and permeability to performance are being studied. Formulation studies examine the effect of thinners, rheology modifiers, de-foamers, and pigments on performance.

MATERIALS RESEARCH CAMPAIGN's Polymer Coatings S&T Footprint	
S&T AREA	**POSTURE**
Polymer Coatings	LEAD

Corrosion & Fatigue research explores corrosion behavior of magnesium and aluminum alloys for structural and protection applications – novel characterization techniques are studied to map corrosion initiation sites and local alloy chemistry; and mitigating fretting fatigue mechanisms in aviation materials to decrease sustainment costs and reduce aviation crashes.

Corrosion Science seeks an understanding of the fundamental processes and mechanistic aspects of material degradation so that intelligent and environmentally friendly solutions to corrosion problems can be developed. This effort utilizes and develops new analytical tools with the ability to determine the initial stages of corrosion - spatially and temporally. The current foci are on the electrochemical characterization and a multiscale modeling approach to predict and understand mechanistic details of corrosion.

Fretting Mitigation investigates the incorporation of residual stress inducing processes, coatings, and lubricants into rotorcraft aviation drive train component systems. These improvements will lengthen the current inspection cycle and lower flight risk while allowing the systems to be driven harder.

MATERIALS RESEARCH CAMPAIGN's Corrosion & Fatigue S&T Footprint	
S&T AREA	**POSTURE**
Corrosion Science	COLLABORATE
Fretting Mitigation	LEAD

Energy Fields Coupled-to-Matter applies physics-based fields (acoustic, electromagnetic, and micro-gravitational) to achieve new properties within materials and new fabrication and integration methods.

Processing examines the effect of energetic fields on the synthesis, processing, and application of materials. The same concepts can be applied to manufacturing science. Current research explores the use of electromagnetic and acoustic fields to enhance bonding of dissimilar materials and improve the repair of components during additive manufacturing (friction stir processing, ultrasonic additive manufacturing, cold spray). In addition, the use of fields often enables manufacturing at lower temperatures and shorter times to promote energy savings for more efficient operation.

Properties apply physics-based fields to achieve a profound influence over microstructure and phase that enables access to phases, structures, and properties not achievable through other means. Current research for protective systems involves application of electromagnetic fields to ceramic materials such as polycrystalline alumina (Al_2O_3) to promote crystallographic alignment of grains in a preferred orientation for fabrication of materials with properties closer to that of single crystals.

Materials Research Campaign's Energy Fields Coupled to Matter S&T Footprint	
S&T AREA	**POSTURE**
Processing	LEAD
Properties	COLLABORATE

SCIENCES-FOR-MANEUVER CAMPAIGN

MISSION: To discover, innovate, and transition S&T enabled capabilities that significantly increase the force effectiveness and global responsiveness of the Army - America's primary ground force.

VISION: Air and ground platforms available to commanders of the Army of 2030 are designed and built that make it possible to rapidly respond to emerging conflicts at any location around the globe. Based on vastly improved materials, logistical support needs of the fighting force are greatly reduced. A globally responsive, lethal, and resilient force serves as a significant deterrent to rising conflict. The desired end state is to leverage the full range of S&T enablers to prepare forces

SCIENCES-FOR-MANEUVER CAMPAIGN PLAN

ARL's research investments in Sciences-for-Maneuver focus on gaining a greater fundamental understanding of advanced mobility technologies that enable innovative vehicles configurations and subsystems architectures – critical to the future Army's movement, sustainment, and maneuverability. Knowledge gained through these research efforts will lead to technologies for the design, fabrication, integration, control, and platforms support that will significantly improve Power Projection Superiority for the Army of 2030.

ARL's Sciences-for-Maneuver Campaign builds on fundamental pillars of science and engineering to conduct research in manned-and-unmanned Army air-and-ground vehicles.

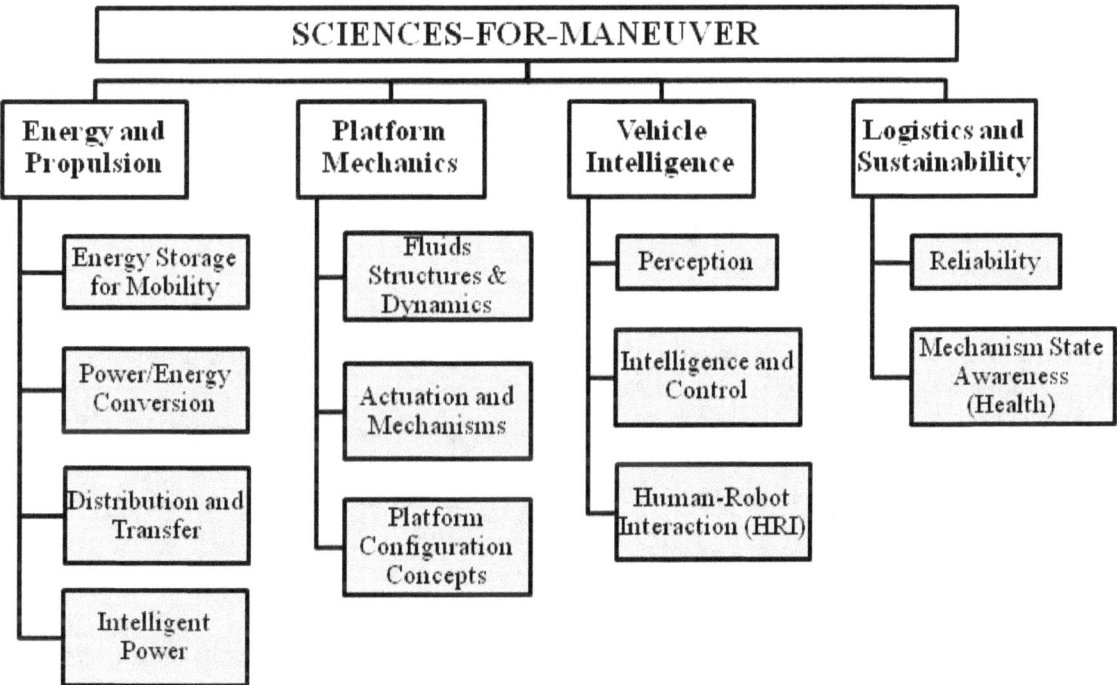

Levels 1 through 3 of the Sciences-for-Maneuver Campaign Plan Taxonomy

ENERGY AND PROPULSION concentrates on understanding and exploiting innovations in mobility, energy sources, storage, generation, conversion, transmission, distribution, and management. The goal of this research is to provide energy power, and propulsion technologies and configurations to enhance the Army operational effectiveness, improve efficiency, and accelerate development of critical military platform systems ensuring Army Power Projection superiority. This concentration area relies on fundamental science research in, and leverages the synergetic link to the Materials Research Campaign.

Energy Storage for Mobility applied research centers on energy storage systems that can be integrated into platforms, Soldiers, and base camps as part on an integral energy system. Energy storage is ubiquitous in Army maneuver efforts, and therefore improved energy storage is an unending challenge. As a Maneuver taxonomy category, *Energy Storage for Mobility* relies on fundamental research in electrochemistry and energy storage synthesis inherent in the Materials Research Campaign. Storage systems enable unique platform operational capabilities; allow improved energy efficiency in platforms and at base camps; and enable extended operations of dismounted Soldiers.

SCIENCES-FOR-MANEUVER CAMPAIGN's Energy Storage for Mobility S&T Footprint	
S&T AREA	**POSTURE**
Energy storage processes, integration, hybridization, and optimization to enable higher storage capacity.	LEAD
Storage devices that can operate at very high voltages in small packages to enable high energy mission systems.	LEAD
Novel energy storage methods toward possible future replacements for chemical energy storage.	LEAD
Advanced packaging techniques.	COLLABORATE
Novel energy storage to fit within acceptable form factors for platforms.	COLLABORATE
Hybrid energy storage systems for unique applications.	COLLABORATE
Energy storage design and packaging	WATCH

Power/Energy Conversion is focused on pursuing the technology necessary to facilitate a motive force and to enable all the systems of a platform as a function of the energy stored in the original source – the fuel or propellant. The available forms of energy during a mission must be converted into kinetic energy and electrical power, and reconverted to other forms of energy. This area also focuses on devices and systems for Soldier energy recharging, and enables the use of renewable energy.

Combustion Science encompasses the characterization, discovery, articulation and modeling the physiological-chemical combustion event relevant to small engine environment.
(i) Coupled Physiochemical Behavior provides fuel property correlation with spray and combustion parameters.
(ii) Elemental Kinetics of Combustion Mechanisms identifies and formulates competing processes in a combustion event.
(iii) Transient Thermal Effects in Finite Combustion States focuses on unveiling the localized thermodynamics states in a closed reacting system.

Multi-phase Fuel Dynamics is focused on discovering new mechanisms to optimize real-time delivery, spray, and dispersion of standard and alternate fuels.
(i) Transient Heavy Fuel Spray and Combustion Characterization and Modeling seeks to understand injection rate dependency of spray and combustion events.
(ii) Quantitative Visualization of High-Pressure Heavy Fuel Spray Combustion develops and couples novel experimental and computational techniques to predict combustion under high-temperature and high pressure conditions.

Compact Power Generation for Lightweight Maneuvers focuses on components innovations to enable future shaft-power generation capabilities for over-matching operational performance space (acoustic signature, range, altitude)
(i) JP-8 Fuel Injector Characterization and Injector Physical Modeling develops scaling law to enable miniaturization of fuel delivery systems
(ii) Lightweight Vehicular Compact Power Components focuses on light-weighting innovations via materials, non-traditional thermal management and active confinement to revolutionize power density.

Turbine and Hybrid Vehicular Power Generation investigates turbomachinery and thermomechanical systems to enable future energy efficient air and ground vehicles while optimizing their maneuverability.
(i) Smart and Adaptable Gas Turbine Blade Research to enable high-temperature, and variable-flow gas turbine engine concepts.

(ii) Novel Concepts for Highly Efficient Compressors and Combustors for efficiency and operability of variable-speed gas turbine concepts.

(iii) Sand-phobic Coatings and Surface Modification to enable gas turbine engine un-inhibited operational performance in extreme impaired environment (including ultra-fine sand, ash and other particles).

SCIENCES-FOR-MANEUVER CAMPAIGN's Power/Energy Conversion S&T Footprint	
S&T AREA	**POSTURE**
Coupled Physiochemical Behavior	LEAD
Elemental Kinetics of Combustion Mechanisms	COLLABORATE
Transient Thermal Effects in Finite Combustion States	LEAD
Transient Heavy Fuel Spray and Combustion Characterization and Modeling	LEAD
Quantitative visualization of High-Pressure Heavy Fuel Spray Combustion	LEAD
JP-8 Fuel Injector Characterization and Injector Physical Modeling	LEAD
Lightweight Vehicular Compact Power Components	LEAD
Smart and Adaptable Gas Turbine Blade Research	LEAD/COLLABORATE
Novel Concepts for Highly Efficient Compressors and Combustors	LEAD/COLLABORATE
Sand-phobic Coatings and Surface Modification	LEAD

Distribution/Transfer focuses on applied research for transmitting and conditioning energy and power into forms for individual systems and components. For mechanical systems, this includes the drive train of the platform; and for electrical systems, this includes switches, converters, inverters and other devices to control and conditioning energy into precise waveforms, frequencies, and voltages for platform mission equipment. For electrical systems, the Materials Research Campaign provides fundamental finding to the Sciences-for-Maneuver Campaign; the Sciences-for-Maneuver Campaign, in turn, provides underlying support to the Sciences for Lethality and Protection Campaign and Information Sciences Campaign as they interface with platforms.

Tribological Physics focuses on understanding the physics and mechanisms leading to high temperature thermomechanical degradation and failures subjected to high-speed loading.

Active Power Transmission Research leverages discoveries in tribology, and materials to improve power density and efficiencies Army vehicles drive systems.

(i) Lightweight Multi-functional Hybrid Gears and Bearings investigates hybrid component technology to reduce drive system weight, noise and vibration

(ii) Probabilistic-Diagnostic Informed Innovations for Power Transmission Light-Weighting focuses on bridging the fundamental physics in materials statistical evolution from manufacturing to fielding leveraging risk and damage tolerance based design methodology in complex transmission systems (planetary, split torque, multi-speed) to reduce weight and size.

SCIENCES-FOR-MANEUVER CAMPAIGN's Distribution/Transfer S&T Footprint	
S&T AREA	**POSTURE**
Tribological Physics	LEAD
Lightweight Multi-functional Hybrid Gears and Bearings	LEAD
Probabalistic-Diagnostic Informed Innovations for Power Transmission Light-weighting	COLLABORATE

Intelligent Power focuses on applied research to achieve the Army goal of energy efficiency through computational control of energy systems. Energy generation, distribution, conversion, and usage can be sensed, communicated and controlled through networked systems. This offers the Army commanders and Soldiers flexibility to achieve multimodal operational flexibility such as efficiency optimization or capability optimization of energy systems. These devices and systems will rely heavily on the Computation Sciences, Information Sciences and Material Research Campaigns for the elemental hardware and software to manage complex energy networks.

Soldier and small system energy is focused on an ensemble of technologies that can power small systems or sensors more efficiently to enable longer duration missions and provide safe and reliable Soldier power that will lower the weight burden while allowing increased mission capabilities. Energy efficient device power architectures that allow the integration of low power sources (harvesting/alternative) with new modes of operation to enable long duration sensing, wearable and conformable hybrid energy sources, wireless energy transfer, microelectormechanical systems based electric components for improved efficiency and swap.

Platform Electrical Architectures focuses on that applied research in systems for generating, distributing, and converting electrical energy from an integrated engineered system to individual mission systems and components. This relies heavily on transitioning technology from fundamental Materials Campaign research, including switches, converters, inverters and other devices to control and conditioning energy into precise waveforms, frequencies and voltages for platform mission equipment, providing underlying support for the objectives and systems of the Sciences for Lethality and Protection Campaign and Computational Sciences Campaign as they interface with platforms.

Power enabled Platform Protection research is focused on pulsed-power components and systems research that improve the reliability and efficiency of pulsed-power components for applications such as electromagnetic armor, electronic fuze initiators, and electronic protection systems.

Vehicle and Platform Power Integration and Control research will evaluate the configuration of electronic components and control strategies required to achieve high-power density and high efficiency power utilization in current and future platform sub-systems, vehicle, and tactical energy network (ad-hoc small scale micro-grid) applications to include the operation of military-specific power distribution topologies at the system and circuit levels.

Base Camp Power Architectures focuses on applied research achieving Army goals of a more fuel efficient method of providing base camp power is required. This area will focus on energy efficiency through autonomous control of tactical base camp energy systems. The systems applied in this area will rely heavily on the Computational Sciences, Information Sciences, and Materials Research Campaigns for that fundamental hardware and software to manage complex energy networks.

SCIENCES-FOR-MANEUVER CAMPAIGN's Intelligent Power S&T Footprint	
S&T AREA	**POSTURE**
Soldier and small system energy	COLLABORATE
Vehicle and Platform Electrical Architectures	COLLABORATE
Power enabled Platform Protection	COLLABORATE

| Vehicle and Platform power integration and control | COLLABORATE |
| Base Camp Power Architectures | COLLABORATE |

PLATFORM MECHANICS focuses on fundamental research that enables the development of the highly maneuverable platforms for the Army of the future. The research is expected to impact a wide array of Army vehicle systems, cutting across the ground, air, and maritime domains, as well as vehicle scales from large to micro-scale devices.

Fluids, Structures & Dynamics research focuses on manned and unmanned air and ground platforms as well as microsystem platforms interact with the environment and how internal components interact with each other. It includes research in fluid dynamics and, more specifically, aerodynamics, where concerns for flow control, interactional aerodynamics effects and multiphase flows are addressed from a maneuver perspective. Aerodynamics interests for the Army range from viscous, extremely low-speed flows for flapping wings to low-and high-subsonic flows over aircraft and slow projectiles to supersonic flows over high speed munitions. Additionally, the fluid-structure interactions associated with micro air vehicles, parachutes, and aeroelasticity issues are addressed. Structural dynamics includes loads and vibration of structures and mitigation technologies such as tuning frequencies, damping, or absorbers. Vehicle dynamics, research is focused on the control response times, stability, and handling qualities of the platform in steady state and during maneuvers, as well as the flight mechanics of air vehicles (the science associated with the propulsion rotating systems, rocket motors, and propeller and rotor blade systems) are also of interest in this area. Acoustics research focuses on sources of noise on the system and covers the noise generation and propagation from the platform for the purpose of sound mitigation of the maneuver. Finally, terramechanics is the study of the interaction between a platform and the ground, particularly when the ground is a non-solid surface such as sand, mud, or snow.

Fluid Dynamics (Aerodynamics) research interests for the Army include viscous, extremely low-speed flows for flapping wings, low-and high-subsonic flows over aircraft and slow projectiles, and supersonic flows over high speed munitions and platforms.
(i) Aerodynamic Interactions in Ducted Rotor Systems research focuses on interactions of blade tip vortices with structures and flow separation off the duct inlet and diffuser.
(ii) Fluid Dynamics of Flapping Wings research focuses on generation, evolution and stability of the leading edge vortex and exploitation of the vortex for aerodynamic performance improvements.
(iii) Aerodynamic Flow Control-Thermoacoustic Excitation Research explores new flow control approaches that could enable effective control under conditions in which traditional instability based approaches fall short.
(iv) Unsteady Aerodynamics for Handheld Aerial Mobility research focuses on exploring the relative efficiency and control of micro-air devices propelled by various bio-inspired and non-bio inspired concepts.

Fluid Structure Interaction research investigates aeroelasticity issues associated with air vehicles, and parachutes to improve their performance.
(i) Fluid membrane interactions research focuses on the modeling of highly flexible membranes and their interaction with the flow. Novel computational techniques to deviate from traditional computational gridding approaches will be investigated. This concentration area also relies on capabilities in the Computational Sciences Campaign.
(ii) Morphing Structures research explores morphing of structures as a mechanism to alter the performance of flight vehicles including range, endurance, speed, payload, and maneuverability.

Structural Dynamics research addresses dynamic stability, vibration, and damping of deformable and moving parts within a system or component. This includes forced vibration, resonance, active and passive damping, vibration suppression, and stability. It includes dynamics and elastic deformations of joints, beams, rods, plates, shells, and other structural members and parts.

Vehicle and Multibody Dynamics research is focused on the control response times, stability, and handling qualities of the platform during maneuvers, as well as the flight mechanics of air vehicles. The research also focuses on better understanding of the dynamic theory and modeling tools for propulsion rotating systems, rocket motors, and propeller and rotor blade systems.

(i) Surface Interactions for Systems Employing Unique Mobility Research looks to create and validate physics-based dynamic simulations of mechanical systems employing unique modes of mobility and manipulation and their interaction with surfaces and objects in the environment.

(ii) Control of a Quadrupedal Platform Research explores actuation and control of a dynamic quadrupedal robot with a flexible actuated spine through simulation and validation through experimentation with hardware. The research seeks to understand and demonstrate the contribution of an actuated flexible spine to the efficiency of a dynamic gait.

(iii) Self-Righting a Generic Robot Research focuses on better understanding the link between a robot's morphology and its ability to self-right. It also includes application of developed algorithms to fielded systems.

(iv) Navigation in Constrained Space Research addresses the development of methodologies and algorithms to enable unmanned air systems to safely navigate in complex 3-D environments with constrained space and perform a task in which there is physical interaction with the environment.

Aeromechanics/Flight Mechanics research addresses the performance and dynamics of vehicles and systems in the presence of air. It combines the separate disciplines of structural dynamics, aerodynamics, and flight dynamics for the aerial platform systems, subsystems and components. For aircraft and munitions, it encompasses aspects related to performance, including lift, drag, system trim in steady state and maneuvering flight, and power required. These are necessary to study more global system properties such as flight mechanics and mission effectiveness. Aeromechanics also includes aeroelastic stability of the vehicle and its component parts, such as wings, fins, control surfaces, propulsion systems, and rotor blades, and interactional aerodynamics between these parts of the system. Flight mechanics encompasses control, trim, stability, and handling qualities for air vehicles and munitions. Flight mechanics addresses full six-Degrees-of-Freedom (DoF) trim and stability. Handling qualities research focuses on ensuring adequate power and control for maneuvers and reducing pilot workload to perform maneuvers and other piloting tasks.

(i) Rotorcraft Autorotation Simulation Research focuses on development of modeling capability for rotorcrafts after a partial or total loss of power and calculating the optimal path to follow to minimize ground impact or return to base using remaining engine(s).

(ii) Active Rotor Technologies is a broad thrust area that combines several active structure or flow control technologies. Some of these technologies are active devices on rotor blade such as trailing edge flap for aeromechanic performance improvements, vibration reduction and noise control.

(iii) Aeroelastic/Aeromechanical Stability research focuses on development of novel

structural, dynamic, and/or aerodynamic concepts, computational modeling, and wind tunnel aeroelastic stability testing.

(iv) CFD/CSD Tools & Analytical Techniques research focuses on modeling advanced configurations and new technologies with CFD/CSD, as well as improving modeling fidelity for legacy and new aircraft.

Acoustics research focuses on development of noise sources identification and mitigation in platforms as well as the propagation through the systems and subsystems to provide stealthy maneuver.

(i) Computational Aeroacoustics Rotor Systems efforts involve computing the aerodynamic flowfield to determine acoustics sources and noise propagation. The aerodynamics coupling with the elastic deformations of rotor blades is a major focus area which includes modeling the structural dynamics of the blade.

(ii) Flame Extinction Using Forced Flow research explores the feasibility of nonchemical fire suppression acoustic waves. The research investigates theoretical and experimental methods, to understand flame extinction using continuous and oscillating flow.

(iii) Vehicle Acoustic Signature Control Research entails identification, characterization, and categorization of non-mechanical methods to counteract/cancel the low-frequency, high energy, minimal attenuation components of sound pressure oscillations. Additionally, the research looks to characterize the acoustic absorbing properties of nanostructured materials, or composites with nanomaterial inclusions, and to investigate the sound-dampening effects of such nanomaterials applied to vehicle structures.

Nonlinear Dynamics and Stability research focuses on high-dimensional systems in which physically intuitive frameworks that derive from the intersection of differential geometry and dynamical systems are ill-equipped to handle. New approaches for decompositions and stability characterization of nonlinear systems are conceived of and developed from canonical contexts up to demonstration in platform mechanics problems in which viable approaches have yet to be developed.

SCIENCES-FOR-MANEUVER CAMPAIGN's Mechanics, Fluid Structures, and Dynamics S&T Footprint	
S&T AREA	**POSTURE**
Aerodynamic Interactions in Ducted Rotor Systems	COLLABRATE
Fluid Dynamics of Flapping Wings	LEAD
Aerodynamic Flow Control-Thermoacoustic Excitation	LEAD
Unsteady Aerodynamics for Handheld Aerial Mobility	LEAD
Fluid membrane interactions	LEAD
Morphing Structures	LEAD
Surface Interactions for Systems Employing Unique Mobility	LEAD
Control of a Quadrupedal Platform	COLLABORATE
Self-Righting a Generic Robot	LEAD
Navigation in Constrained Space	COLLABORATE
Rotorcraft Autorotation Simulation	LEAD
Aeromechanics of Active Rotor Flap	LEAD
Aeroelastic/Aeromechanical Stability	LEAD
CFD/CSD Tools & Analytical Techniques	LEAD

Computational Aeroacoustics Predictions of Rotor Systems	LEAD
Flame Extinction Using Forced Flow	COLLABORATE
Vehicle Acoustic Signature Control	LEAD
Bifurcations and Instabilities in High Dimensional Nonlinear Systems	LEAD
Control & Flight Dynamics for MicroUAS	LEAD
Terra Mechanics	COLLABORATE

Actuation and Mechanisms research focuses on the physical movement of a platform including the control surfaces and linkages, such as those currently required to move the rotor blade system on a helicopter, the propulsors, and other actuators or manipulators. Additionally, active control and multibody interactions from the mechanical perspective are considered.

Active Control focuses on non-traditional means of feedback control including systems utilizing distributed actuation, sensing and computation to address low level vehicle control.

Reconfigurable structures research focuses on concepts on self-healing capabilities for enhanced autonomous durability using micro-encapsulation technique. These research efforts concentrate on overcoming these challenges and look for a potential new process for new types of active, reconfigurable materials and structures with the potential to redirect energy and load paths to enable structural morphing and healing, vibration attenuation, and dynamic load mitigation. Research efforts also focus on capabilities for multifunctional structures, which not only are capable of carrying loads but also potentially sense materials damage precursors, harvest and store energy, for use in sensing, actuation, and overall maneuver sustainment.

Propulsors research focuses on flight vehicle control and "smart" systems design, greater understandings of unsteady aerodynamic phenomena, such as high alpha dynamic separation, vortex shedding, control surface/vortex interaction, divert thruster/vehicle interaction, roll control stability and propulsion system integration.

Manipulation research explores autonomous self-righting, throwing, grasping moving objects, and grasping an object while moving.

Actuation research of interest includes non-traditional transduction mechanism which might have dual actuation and sensing capabilities or integrate cleanly into a structural member rather than being a discrete component. The intended applications extending from directly performing work in a system to enabling locomotion to modulating the stiffness of a component. Research spans the disciplines of chemical, biological, and materials-level actuation through multi-body/component research of complex mechanisms. It encompasses micro to human or larger physical scales.
(i) Actuation Sensing & Electromechanical Logic Research explores non-traditional actuation/sensing mechanisms scaled for micro-air vehicles
(ii) Magnetostrictive (MS) Material and Platform Crashworthiness Modeling looks to develop and validate models for analysis and design of MS actuators and sensors and to discover and implement advanced actuator and sensor technology using MS materials including Rotary magneto-rheological EA (MREA) with magnetic bias, and Magneto-strictive Friction EA (MFEA). Applications include items such as novel seat energy absorbers for enhanced active vehicle safety.

SCIENCES-FOR-MANEUVER CAMPAIGN's Actuation and Mechanisms S&T Footprint	
S&T AREA	**POSTURE**
Neuromorphic Control	LEAD
Reconfigurable blades	LEAD
Control & Flight Dynamics for Micro Unmanned Aerial Systems	LEAD
Grasping Using Astrictive Means	LEAD
Actuation Sensing & Electromechanical Logic	LEAD
Magnetostrictive Material and Platform Crashworthiness Modeling	LEAD

Platform Configuration Concepts research examines advanced methods and tools for design and assessment of concept vehicles. The focus is on enhancing certainty, expanding capability, and exploring revolutionary interactive environments in support of early conceptual design of ground vehicles, fixed wing aircraft, and rotary wing aircraft. The research is not limited to the vehicle system; it extends down to component-level technologies and up to operation, maintenance, and sustainment activities driven by diverse, complex environments.

Design Decision Science research focuses on gaining a fundamental understanding and identification of decision science, multi-criteria decision analysis (MCDA), and hardware-software allocation optimization.

(i) Aerial Delivery Optimization Software research has two complementary parts: a) explore strategic decision making across responsiveness, efficiency, and cost of military aerial resupply for humanitarian assistance/disaster relief (HA/DR); and b) explore decision making across effectiveness and cost of one class of precision airdrop delivery systems (PADS).

(ii) Functional Allocation Trades Between Hardware and Software research is exploring system-level optimization using multi-level objective functions and constraints as an enabler. Manual and automatic component allocation approaches are being sought, with system-level measures of utility used for assessment of alternatives defined by multiple hardware/software components.

Technology Tradespace Exploration research focuses on technology modeling, technology insertion analysis, statistical data analysis, interactive exploration and reasoning, and visual analytics.

(i) Rotorcraft Capability Assessment and Tradeoff Environment (CATE) research applies conceptual-level tradespace analysis and decision science to explore tradeoffs between requirements, technologies, and design parameters. The environment relies on surrogate modeling and visual, interactive exploration to identify important technology research areas early in design, and creates multi-objective optimal portfolios of specific and notional technologies.

(ii) Bio Inspired Air Vehicle with Arbitrary Wing Kinematics research is to develop a new, highly customizable platform capable of adjustment to body pose and flapping position and speed. The vehicle provides a platform that is capable of free flight using separately actuated and controlled wings, a unique capability. This platform will enable a new level of understanding for reconfigurable flapping wing vehicles by illuminating the importance of subsystem interaction, flapping kinematics, and component matching.

(iii) Open MDAO-based framework for Optimization and Sensitivity research is exploiting multidisciplinary design and optimization methods for applications in rotorcraft design and analysis.

Capability Based Assessment research focuses on whole system tradeoffs, capability and performance modeling, resilient system architectures, system concepts, and lifecycle capability and cost analysis.

(i) Tunable Stiffness Flapping Mechanism research is exploring the benefits of including compliant energy storage elements in small flapping mechanisms. Due to the tight constraints on payload at small sizes, such an innovation will allow for increased usefulness by reducing reliance on heavy batteries to sustain flight. A model is under development that will capture the results of experimental trials and enable future designers to include compliant elements for energy savings.

(ii) Mission-Driven Microsystem Design and Validation research is exploring advanced design methodologies for micro autonomous systems that can improve military battlespace awareness. An objective is to enable in situ rapid manufacturing of unmanned aerial ISR platforms using a minimal set of components and 3D printing technology. A technology assessment framework synthesizes candidate families of vehicles based on mission scenarios, measures of effectiveness, mission functions, and technology descriptions. A combination of virtual and physical experimental is used for verification and validation.

(iii) Evaluating Component Interactions Within Complex Systems research is exploring methods, processes, and tools to identify and visualize interactions and dependencies between the components of a complex system, and between the system and its environment. An interactive environment will enable exploration of the behavior of a complex system, identify undesirable interactions, alert the user, and aid the user in averting interactions.

SCIENCES-FOR-MANEUVER CAMPAIGN's Platform Configuration Concepts S&T Footprint	
S&T AREA	**POSTURE**
Aerial Delivery Optimization	LEAD
Functional Allocation Trades Between Hardware and Software	COLLABORATE
Rotorcraft Capability Assessment and Tradeoff Environment research	COLLABORATE
Bio Inspired Air Vehicle With Arbitrary Wing Kinematics	COLLABORATE
Open MDAO based framework for Optimization and Sensitivity	LEAD
Tunable Stiffness Flapping Mechanism	COLLABORATE
Mission-Driven Microsystem Design and Validation	COLLABORATE
Evaluating Component Interactions Within Complex Systems	COLLABORATE

VEHICLE INTELLIGENCE focuses on fundamental research that enables effective teaming of Soldiers and unmanned vehicles to conduct maneuver and military missions. ARL's activities are centered on enhancing the autonomous capabilities of unmanned systems. This research thrust compliments research conducted within the Information Sciences Campaign, but focuses exclusively on vehicle systems in real world environments.

Perception research examines the vehicle's "understanding" of its own state and that of its local environment, in the context of its mission, background knowledge, and organic sensor information. It includes research on specialized sensors and concomitant processing; distributed perception to enable navigation and manipulation of extremely small platforms; and vehicle planning and monitoring behaviors supported through combined sensory and contextual information in a world model.

Sensing & Sensor Processing is focused on the sensors and low level processing, organic to the vehicle that enables it to sense both static and dynamic objects in its local environment.

Modalities range across the electromagnetic spectrum, including radar, IR and visible imagery, and beyond to include acoustic or tactile sensing. Imaging sensors can provide information in a single dimension (range), two-dimensional (azimuth and elevation), or three-dimensional (azimuth, elevation, and range). It includes initial signal processing, segmentation of imagery into distinct elements, and fusion of data from multiple sensors

(i) Hardware Accelerated Lidar Processing research focuses on LIDAR processing registration and segmentation algorithms that are specifically designed for parallel computing.

(ii) Passive Perception in Challenging Scenes research addresses fundamental issues in passive stereo vision. High dynamic range and polarization approaches will be used to significantly improve stereo perception and 3D modeling in scenes that involve high contrast, low-texture, specular, and transmissive surfaces.

(iii) Compressed Sensing LADAR research exploits the concept of compressed sensing to LADAR and expects to reduce size, weight, and power of such systems to a fraction of state-of-the-art baselines

(iv) Improved Contact Sensor for Terrain Classification and Grasping: creates terrain contact sensors intended for legged robots

(v) Passive Multi-spectral Sensing research is focused on creating a passive multispectral imaging (MSI) system. Multispectral data will be fused with a 3-D point cloud generated by LADAR

(vi) Short-range sensing for Dexterous Manipulation and Unique Mobility extends research on using a laser line stripe-based triangulation sensors for 3-D perception to detect and classify objects made of materials with non-Lambertian reflectance properties, such as glass, metal, or translucent materials, which are difficult challenges for perception systems.

(vii) High Performance Visual Range and Motion Estimation for Small Platforms extends a compact, forward-looking 3-D perception system based on stereo vision to provide 360°, 3-D situational awareness, including the ability to maintain an accurate map in the presence of moving objects and to detect and track nearby moving objects, such as personnel or other vehicles.

Semantic Perception (Scene Understanding) takes sensed data from one or multiple sources segments and/or coalesces data into structures that can be labeled as objects in space or through tracking in successive scans/frames (temporal sequence) into actionsn. The labeling process can consider external information or situational context. Labeling of the objects provides representations that can be utilized in abstract reasoning for situational awareness, behavior planning, execution, and monitoring. The dynamic nature of military operations places a strong emphasis upon learning from sparse datasets.

(i) Landmark based navigation research is focused on landmark based navigation algorithms using novelty recognition to allow for localization in a GPS-denied environment.

(ii) Semantic Spatial Understanding research focuses on mechanisms to infer the purpose of an object or space based upon labeling of the object from sensory data, contextual information, supervised and unsupervised learning

(iii) Primed Perception research is focused on using contextual information to improve the perceptual capabilities of unmanned systems.

(iv) Uncertainty of Semantic Labeling and Semantic Object research focuses on the uncertainty arising from imperfect semantic labeling in order to achieve robust behaviors, as well as uncertainty inherent in the different types of sensors leading to the multi-hypothesis architecture of the Common World Model.

(v) Building Facade, Window, and Door Detection research is focused on creating detection algorithms for key descriptors in outdoor urban environments, considering range of variation of these purpose-built features through the range of operational urban environments.

(vi) 3D Object Detection and Pose Estimation research is focused on creating algorithms for estimation of pose and tracking over time.

Distributed Perception/Fusion research is focused on utilizing raw data from multiple, possibly heterogeneous, spatially and/or temporally dispersed sources and combines the data to categorize or identify scene elements, including objects and or actions, and the relationships, e.g., relative position, between those scene elements. This process is often required due to the limited capabilities of the sensors, such that when combined with contextual information, the resultant quality far exceeds that of the individual sensor feeds. The potentially heterogeneous nature of the sensed data places a significant emphasis upon correlation of data possessing different resolution and sensitivity.

World Model research is focused on creating an environment which joins metric, semantic, and cognitive data levels through a data store, access APIs, runtime framework, and complete documentation

SCIENCES-FOR-MANEUVER CAMPAIGN's Perception S&T Footprint	
S&T AREA	**POSTURE**
Hardware Accelerated Lidar Processing	LEAD
Passive Perception in Challenging Scenes	LEAD
Compressed Sensing LADAR	LEAD
Improved Contact Sensor for Terrain Classification and Grasping	LEAD
Passive Multi-spectral Sensing	LEAD
Short-range sensing for Dexterous Manipulation and Unique Mobility	LEAD
High Performance Visual Range and Motion Estimation for Small Platforms	LEAD
Algorithms for object/behavior recognition	COLLABORATE
Mult-sensor fusion algorithms	COLLABORATE
Conventional sensor technology	WATCH
Landmark based navigation	LEAD
Semantic Spatial Understanding	LEAD
Primed Perception	LEAD
Uncertainty of Semantic Labeling and Semantic Objects	LEAD
Building Facade, Window, and Door Detection	LEAD
3D Object Detection and Pose Estimation	LEAD
Common World Model	LEAD

Intelligence and Control research examines vehicle behaviors, including planning, monitoring, and correcting behaviors to achieve desired mission goals. It focuses heavily on mechanisms for learning, both supervised and unsupervised; for continual or life-long learning, and for generalization. Research in this area focuses on effective mechanisms for creating increasingly complex and adaptive *behaviors* from elemental machine skills, capabilities that will enable the vehicle to effectively team with Soldiers and other unmanned vehicles at the operational tempo of the mission. These efforts include the means for creating behaviors for individual vehicles, as well behaviors for groups of homogeneous or heterogeneous vehicles working together to achieve a singular goal. We generally describe the vehicle control architecture as hierarchical and possessing three layers: a low level control layer, a vehicle centric middle layer, and a global mission level layer.

Control focuses on the low level processes or response that closely couple sensing and action (actuation) of individual elements of the vehicle.

Planning/Guidance research focuses on the middle level, vehicle-centric layer of the control architecture, that is dedicated to immediate path planning. It is generally characterized by a metric approach with some form of constraints in which the array of possible actions or paths is characterized by some form of objective (cost) function that may be evaluated for each potential path or a subset. Analysis of alternatives consists of evaluation of this function to determine an appropriate choice of action. The resultant action may be optimal or sub-optimal based upon the degree of analysis permitted by the allotted time which is governed by factors such as the speed of the vehicle and requirement for "real-time" action. The waypoint navigation (semi-autonomous) mode of vehicle operation will interact with this middle layer of the architecture.

Abstract Reasoning places a focus on the cognitive element of the architecture, conducting evaluation of abstract labels and concepts, incorporating contextual knowledge including models of human behavior. As such, it will utilize and evaluate imprecise measures rooted in human. It will place a heavy emphasis upon learning as a means of adapting to complex behaviors and highly dynamic environments. Human-robot teaming, as opposed to human control of robotic assets, will generally occur at this level of the architecture.

(i) Cognitive Robotics Architecture research focuses on cognitive mechanisms and functionality necessary for adaptive and intelligent behavior. These mechanisms, at a minimum, include working memory, long term memory, attention, and perception. These mechanisms must combine, interact, and cooperate with each other in a robust and effective way in order to lay the foundations for intelligent autonomous behavior on the battlefield

(ii) Connecting Cognitive Architectures to Real Robots research combines cognitive reasoning system with semantic perception and natural language-driven tactical behaviors

(iii) Hybrid Integrated Architectures for Prediction research focuses on integration of the Leabra neural architecture with the memory characteristics of the ACT-R symbolic architecture in order to achieve unsupervised learning of new object categories.

(iv) Lifelong Bayesian Cost Models for Dynamic Objects research is focused on using gamma distribution for Bayesian updates to improve route planning techniques.

Teaming & Coordination focuses on the interaction of multiple entities to achieve a specified goal. In the context of military units coordination represents the understanding or deconfliction of independent activities being undertaken by different elements to meet individual or common goals. Teaming focuses upon close interaction among elements to take specific coupled actions that will result in meeting a common goal. These elements may be homogeneous or heterogeneous in form, function, or capability. Communication among elements, either through direct or indirect means, will be critical to the ability to successfully meet goals.

Behaviors are the complex actions of a vehicle (or soldiers) built from a hierarchy of elemental tasks and capabilities to achieve one or more specified goals. When mirrored to the three level control architecture model utilized in the current description of vehicle control, behaviors generally correspond to actions taken at the upper or cognitive level. In teaming between Soldiers and unmanned system a common understanding of vehicle behaviors will facilitate transparency and foster mutual trust.

(i) Tactical Behaviors research is focused on a modular software framework instantiating the Tactical Behavior Specification (TBS) of Intelligence Architecture.

(ii) Lifelong Improvement of the Robustness of Tactical Behaviors research is focuses on reduced order planning approaches to improve performance through experience.

(iii) Tactical Behavior Support research provides several adaptive tactical behaviors and

actions and a richer interface between the low level planner and the world model with feedback, human-robot teaming behaviors, observe and search behaviors as described in Tactical Behavior Specification (TBS).

Learning & Adaptation are key cognitive features of an intelligent vehicle that denote its ability to adjust its actions and/or behavior to successfully achieve goals in dynamic and/ or previously unknown situations and environments. Adaptation generally focuses on the elasticity of flexibility of the control system to achieve success for smaller changes in the operational or physical environment while learning focuses upon the synthesis of behavior to adjust to larger changes in such environments. The latter may be supervised in which another entity provides feedback concerning success or self-supervised (unsupervised) in which the entity itself provides the feedback mechanism through evaluation of outcomes. A key feature of human learning is the ability to recognize success and modify behavior based upon a small number of examples, as opposed to many instances of machine learning which require very large numbers of exemplars.

(i) Robot Mobility Model Formulation and Self Calibration for Improved Estimation and Control research is focused on creating techniques to calibrate vehicle models while the vehicle executes its mission in an arbitrary terrain. Constant parameters are calibrated as well as the statistics of random errors and variations. The latter are for use in machine learning and pose estimation algorithms at all levels in the cognitive architecture

(ii) Anytime Prediction and Anytime Visual Search research is focused on creating techniques that makes machine learning algorithms faster, time budget aware, and able to make predictions under various time budgets at test time.

(iii) Learning Low-Dimensional Manipulation Gestures research is focused on using low-dimensional trajectory features on high-dimensional motion data for analysis and planning.

(iv) Self-Supervised, On-Line Learning for Building and Using Robot/Environment Interaction Models research is focused on algorithms which allow robots to automatically learn complex interactions with its environment—without human supervision—in order to benefit directly from experience.

SCIENCES-FOR-MANEUVER CAMPAIGN's Intelligence and Control S&T Footprint	
S&T AREA	**POSTURE**
Planning under Multiple Hypotheses in Perception	LEAD
Cognitive Robotics Architecture	LEAD
Hybrid Integrated Architectures for Prediction	COLLABORATE
Lifelong Bayesian Cost Models for Dynamic Objects:	LEAD
Shared Topological Representations and Algorithms for Human-Robot Teaming	COLLABORATE
Tactical Behaviors	LEAD
Lifelong Improvement of the Robustness of Tactical Behaviors	LEAD
Tactical Behavior Support	LEAD
Robot Mobility Model Formulation and Self Calibration for Improved Estimation and Control	LEAD
Anytime Prediction and Anytime Visual Search	LEAD
Learning Low-Dimensional Manipulation Gestures	LEAD
Self-Supervised, On-Line Learning for Building and Using Robot/Environment Interaction Models	LEAD

Self-Supervised, On-Line Learning for Building and Using Robot/Environment Interaction Models	LEAD
Learning and reasoning	COLLABORATE
Control technologies	COLLABORATE
Collaborative and team behaviors	COLLABORATE
Planning algorithms	WATCH
Hardware/Firmware development	WATCH

Human-Robot Interaction (HRI) research focuses on interactions between humans and robots/intelligent platforms. It examines mechanisms for effective robot communication between Soldiers and robots; communication or transmittal of information in its most elemental sense – including the understanding of gesture and voice; the use of language as an abstraction for transmitting information; and intra-team behavior. Long term research also includes efforts to measure the human state and explore new architectures that incorporate insight into the operator state and intention in Human/Autonomous System Decision Architectures for the integration of human adaptive abilities for enhanced autonomy in complex and dynamic conditions. Finally, it provides models of societal interaction to enable construction of robot behaviors that will lie within societal behavior norms and create a common model of behavior.

Soldier-Machine Communication revolves around the ability of the vehicle system to understand the multi-modal sensory information provided by soldiers and/or the local populace. Traditionally, direct commands and reporting of vehicle state, through electronic means or otherwise, has been utilized for the control of unmanned systems. More recently there has been an increased emphasis upon voice, gesture, and text, focusing upon the use of natural language as a medium for conveying complex information and commands, to create a more natural information exchange.

Intra-Team Behavior revolves around the ability to create a common, though not necessarily identical, mental model of the world and the decision making processfor both intelligent vehicles and soldiers who are members of a heterogeneous small-unit team. This requires understanding of likely soldier and robot behavior (transparency). It is hypothesized that transparency of action will lead to greater levels of Soldier robot trust together with more effective communication and control.

Societal Interaction focuses on understanding collaborative human-robot interactions in complex operational environments including interactions between vehicle systems and the indigenous population. This includes development of models for human interaction to include social cues both verbal and non-verbal that provide context and facilitate direct interaction. Thus it will provide valuable contextual information for utilization in both perception and machine intelligence.

SCIENCES-FOR-MANEUVER CAMPAIGN's Human-Robot Interaction (HRI) S&T Footprint	
S&T AREA	**POSTURE**
Autonomous Squad Member	LEAD
Common Ground for Military Operations	LEAD
Manned-Unmanned Teaming	COLLABORATE
Trust	COLLABORATE
Transparency	COLLABORATE

| Multi-modal human-robot communication | COLLABORATE |
| Operator Control Units/Interface elements | WATCH |

LOGISTICS AND SUSTAINABILITY focuses on fundamental and applied research to enable the rapid and accurate assessment of existing and future Army platform's components, systems, sub-systems, and accessories health status, usage and readiness to provide unmatched maneuvers, affordability, reliability, and availability.

Reliability research focuses on exploring and innovating capabilities and design concepts for durability and fatigue mitigations and preventions that can be used to optimize redundancy for fail safe taking into account reliability metrics, and achieve the "zero-maintenance" goal for Army platform systems, subsystems, and components. The long-term research aims at achieving ultra-high reliability for Army future platforms.

Damage Tolerance and Durability research efforts aim at reducing platform structural component weights, increasing strength, extending life-cycle, understanding of fatigue root causes, and advancing 3-D printing capabilities to produce "fatigue-free" structural components. This focus area includes fundamental research to quantify initial crack characteristics and advance computational methodologies for determining stress intensity factors, fatigue life prediction, and effects of fatigue life enhancement methods on fatigue life of dynamic components. It also covers fatigue-crack-growth experimentation to develop threshold stress intensity factors to be used in the design of Army vehicles.

(i) Extremely Lightweight, Adaptive, Durable, and Damage Tolerant (XLADD) Structures focuses on discovering, innovating, demonstrating, and transitioning capabilities and technologies to produce XLADD structural components, which exhibit "fatigue-free" characteristics. This thrust area also relies on fundamental research in the Materials Research Campaign.

(ii) High Strength Structures establishes and demonstrates novel concepts and design methodologies enabled by advances in high strength materials development to enable durable and lightweight vehicle. This concentration area also leverages the synergetic link to the Materials Research Campaign.

(iii) 3-D Printing of "Fatigue-Free" Structures focuses on the fabrication of multifunctional nanocomposite components by 3-D printing that displays hierarchical ordering capable of eliminating traditional material property trade-off relations such as strength and toughness, strength and density, hardness and ductility to enhance fatigue-resistance.

Physics of Fatigue research focuses on gaining a fundamental understanding and identification of the root causes of system and component failure. The goal is to identify failure modes, rank potential factors contributing to each failure mode, confirm the root causes of the failures, and determine their effects on the subsystem and systems. This research explores capabilities for early detection of material damage precursor, how fast it evolves, and at what point in time it can be mitigated to prevent the impending catastrophic failure of structures. Furthermore, the efforts incorporate physical models capable of encompassing scale dependent mechanisms leading to a new framework for fatigue life estimation based on total health state awareness.

Maintenance-Free Systems research efforts focus on concepts for self healing and reconfiguration technologies to regain platform required capabilities to perform mission maneuvers without substantial needs for maintenance, inspections, and manual repairs. The research is dedicated to manipulating chemical, mechanical, electrical, fluidic, and magnetic properties of structural and dynamic components to improve their reliability without requiring maintenance.

(i) Maintenance-free Structural Components focuses on concepts for self diagnostics and inspections to reduce structural components sustainment costs substantially.

(ii) Maintenance-free Dynamics Components focuses on concepts for self inspections to substantially reduce sustainment costs for dynamics components such as drive train, propulsion systems and rotor systems.

SCIENCES-FOR-MANEUVER CAMPAIGN's Reliability S&T Footprint	
S&T AREA	**POSTURE**
Extremely Lightweight, Adaptive, Durable, and Damage Tolerant Structures	COLLABORATE
High Strength Structures	COLLABORATE
3-D Printing of "Fatigue-Free" Structures	COLLABORATE
Fatigue Tolerant, Concepts, Computation, and Technologies	COLLABORATE
Independent Load Path/Fail Safe	WATCH
Canary Concepts for Structural Components	WATCH
Self-Healing Structural Components	COLLABORATE
Maintenance-free Structural Components	LEAD
Maintenance-free Dynamics Components	COLLABORATE
Maintenance-free Systems/Sub-Systems and Accessories	WATCH

Mechanism State Awareness (Health) research focuses on discovering, innovating, and transitioning capabilities and design concepts that can be used to enable state-of-the-art self-health diagnostics, inspections and monitoring for platform systems, subsystems, and components. These research efforts include built-in state awareness, prognostics and diagnostics, probabilitics and risk assessment, and load monitoring and regime recognition. The long term goal of this S&T thrust is to enable the development, demonstration, and transition of the Virtual Risk-informed Agile Maneuver Sustainment (VRAMS) technology to substantially reduce the Army sustainment costs and to provide the Army commanders with the capability to plan missions in real time. This concentration area also relies on capabilities in, and leverages the synergetic link to the Information Sciences and Computational Sciences Campaigns.

Built-in State Awareness research efforts aim at enabling the capabilities and technologies to provide self diagnostics and inspection to reduce vehicles maintenance, increase the Army platform availability and sustain them at low costs *(i) Virtual Risk-informed Agile Maneuver Sustainment (VRAMS)* provides capabilities for capturing platform health information at the material level, executing multi-scale modeling as well as risk assessment in real time, and providing damage/ load-based reconfigurable operational maneuver solutions to keep the actual loading at or below the acceptable threshold to sustain "fatigue-free" platforms with little or zero-maintenance.

(ii) Material Damage Precursors Identification and Detection explores intelligent built-in sensing capabilities and technologies to capture or detect materials damage precursors prior to the onset of potential degradations including cracks.

Prognostics and Diagnostics (P&D) research efforts aims at providing capabilities to accurately determine the remaining useful life of systems or components. The prognostics research intends to focus on improving the accuracy of predicting the time at which a system or a component will no longer perform its intended function. The diagnostics research focuses on fault detection, isolation, and identification when it occurs in a system or component.

(i) Structural Health Monitoring (SHM) innovates monitoring capabilities to examine the health and degradation in structural components.

(ii) SHM-Non-Destructive Inspection (NDI) Correlation establishes the relationships between data collected from SHM and NDI to determine the accuracy of SHM and applicability of SHM information toward determining the remaining useful life of structural components.

(iii) Usage-based Remaining Useful Life (RUL) determines the actual damages based on how the platforms are being used to conduct mission and then compute the remaining useful life of platform structures, dynamics/drive-train components, or propulsion/engine systems.

(iv) Mechanical/Structural Diagnostics Research Using Unmanned System seeks to simulate the actual maneuver condition of manned systems to demonstrate innovated P&D capabilities and technologies prior to technology demonstration on manned systems.

Probabilistic and Risk Assessment focuses on leveraging computational capabilities, develop uncertainty quantification and risk mitigation predictions based collected data or information, infer its probable cause, formulate calibrated predictions, assess risk levels, and make an effective and intelligent decision.

Load Monitoring & Regime Recognition research efforts aim at determining actual loading conditions through advanced direct or indirect maneuver recognition measurements.

SCIENCES-FOR-MANEUVER CAMPAIGN's Mechanism State Awareness (Health) S&T Footprint	
S&T AREA	**POSTURE**
Virtual Risk-informed Agile Maneuver Sustainment (VRAMS)	COLLABORATE
Intelligent Built-in Sensing Network for Platform Structures, Mechanical & Drive-Train Components, Propulsion/Engine Systems	COLLABORATE
Intelligent Data Fusion	WATCH
Material Damage Precursors Identification and Detection	COLLABORATE
Structural Health Monitoring (SHM)	COLLABORATE
SHM-NDI Correlation	LEAD
Usage-based Remaining Useful Life (RUL)	LEAD and COLLABORATE
Mechanical/Structural Diagnostics Research Using Unmanned Systems	LEAD
Real-time Risk Assessment for VRAMS	LEAD
Probabilistic Sustainment of Platform Structures, Mechanical & Drive-Train Components, Propulsion/Engine Systems	COLLABORATE
Load-based Reconfigurable Operational Maneuver	COLLABORATE
Advanced Health and Usage Monitoring	COLLABORATE
Intelligent Maneuver Recognition & Mapping	COLLABORATE

INFORMATION SCIENCES CAMPAIGN

MISSION: *To discover, innovate, and transition S&T capabilities that (1) facilitate the availability and effective use of high assurance and high quality information and knowledge at the tactical edge in a timely manner; and (2) facilitate the development of offensive information systems to limit adversary command-and-control capabilities.*

VISION: *Intelligent information systems available to the Army of 2030 provide reliable, timely, valuable, and trustworthy information and knowledge at the most appropriate force echelon, especially to the tactical edge – significantly mitigating tactical surprise. Army offensive information systems significantly limit the adversary's command-and-control capabilities. Intelligent information systems support and team with the force, forming an underlying socio-technical base for all things in the battlespace, from munitions targeting to maneuver to command-and-control. The desired end state is to leverage the range of S&T enablers to prepare forces to succeed in distributed operations and increasingly complex environments where information plays an ever increasing role.*

INFORMATION SCIENCES CAMPAIGN PLAN

ARL's S&T investments in Information Sciences are focused on gaining a greater understanding of emerging technology opportunities that support intelligent information systems that perform acquisition, analysis, reasoning, decision-making, collaborative communication, and assurance of information and knowledge. Understanding gained through these research efforts will lead to technological developments that make it possible to manage and utilize information flows in the battlespace. Technologies resulting from these efforts will have a direct impact on the Information Supremacy of the Army of 2030.

ARL's Information Sciences Campaign builds on fundamental pillars of networks; advanced decision support aids; modeling and simulation of complex environments; and high performance computing to conduct research in areas including *Intelligent Agents; Enhanced Tactical Networks; Effective Decision Support Aids; Knowledge Exploitation; and Cyber Defense and Forensics.*

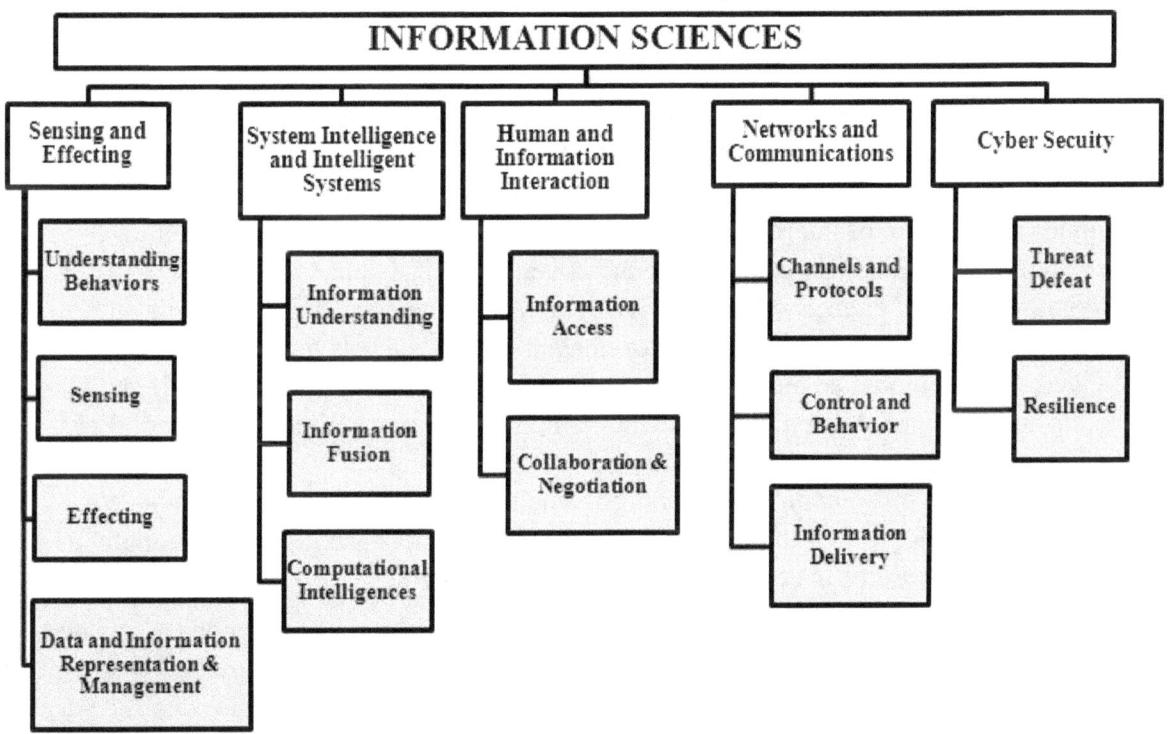

Levels 1 through 3 of the Information Sciences Campaign Plan Taxonomy

SENSING AND EFFECTING research concentrates on understanding and exploiting information gained through sensing and exploiting data to drive effectors. Both sensing and effecting necessitate detailed understanding of corresponding physical behaviors that generate and utilize data, as well as effective means for storage, retrieval, and manipulation of data.

Understanding Phenomenology and Behaviors focuses on gaining a fundamental understanding of the physical and social phenomena and and their impact on relevant measurement tools, and provides the foundation for the effective exploitation of all manifestations of a particular object or activity.

Electromagnetic phenomenology deals with understanding the characteristics of reflected or emitted EM waves, or static electric and magnetic fields associated with physical objects and events of interest.

(i) Device forensics for Electronic Warfare is concerned with developing a methodology for understanding how RF waves couple into electronic circuits. It requires target analysis that includes device features, schematics and chip selection. This is then followed with susceptibility experiments for developing smart modulation parameters for RF injection.

(ii) Modeling of target and clutter radar signature focuses on physics based computational approaches to understand reflected radar intensities of Army targets and clutter objects as a function of polarization, frequency and incidence angle.

(iii) Modeling of RF propagation in high clutter environments focuses on understanding the effects of scattering and propagation from a dense collection of confounding objects, such as in urban areas for example, on radar measurement and eventually on the ability to distinguish real targets from clutter.

(iv) Modeling and simulation of E&B fields investigates mathematical and computational methods for accurate rendering of electric and magnetic fields as a function of object distributions and individual object attributes such as mass, shape, and orientation.

Optical & photonic phenomenology is concerned with properties of interactions of light with objects and their effect on related measurements.

(i) Atmospheric effects on transmission deals with the study of the effect of atmospheric phenomena on the sensed data such as turbulence on image formation.

(ii) Color & other spectral signatures of targets & backgrounds studies reflectances of targets and background objects as a function of incident wavelength ranging principally from the long wave infrared through visible light; on occasion, wavelengths in the ultraviolet region are of interest. Knowledge of spectral characteristics can lead to accurate classification of targets and ground cover.

(iii) Spatiotemporal characteristics of moving objects in video is concerned with understanding space and time behavior of imaged objects such as humans and vehicles in video so that automated algorithms can subsequently provide accurate identification of objects and behavior. Attributes of interest include but are not limited to object outlines, object track characteristics and orientation.

(iv) Identification of chem/bio objects is concerned with determining presence of chemical and biological entities in any of the solid, liquid or gaseous states through their characteristic signatures in scattering or transmission spectra.

Mechanical wave phenomenology covers understanding of wave phenomena associated with vibrations propagating through material, media and physical structures.

(i) Modeling & simulation of acoustic propagation through the atmosphere and seismic propagation through the ground investigates mathematical models and simulation tools that provide realistic characterization of acoustic wave propagation as a function of ambient conditions such as temperature, humidity etc. as well as, refraction, absorption, ground impedance, and multipath.

(ii) Acoustic experimentation studies investigate propagation channel characterization with physical measurements with the aim of enhancing sensor performance and noise mitigation.

Weather phenomenology focuses on assessing the physical state of the atmosphere and its effects on Soldiers, systems and operations

(i)Prediction and characterization of fine scale atmospheric conditions deals with the study of models and techniques that enable estimation of distribution of atmospheric parameters at highly localized physical locations.

(ii) Atmospheric effects on hazardous aerosols studies changes to aerosol signatures caused by exposure to heat, humidity and ultraviolet radiation in the outdoor environment. Secondarily, it also involves studying changes to toxicity and biological viability.

Object interactions with environment phenomenology pertains to studying the effect of attributes of physical objects and their dynamical behavior on measured physical quantities
(i) E&B field interactions with objects & environment studies localized and aggregated field distributions resulting from collections of objects in various environments; a secondary objective may be the influence of the E&B fields on objects of interest.
(ii) Acoustic wave interactions with the environment including physical objects such as terrain, or structures.

INFORMATION SCIENCES CAMPAIGN's Understanding Phenomenology and Behaviors S&T Footprint	
S&T AREA	**POSTURE**
Prediction and characterization of fine scale atmospheric conditions	LEAD
Atmospheric effects on hazardous aerosols	COLLABORATE
Device forensics for Electronic Warfare	WATCH
Modeling of target and clutter radar signature	LEAD
Modeling of RF propagation in high clutter environments	LEAD
Modeling & simulation of E&B Fields; interactions with objects & environment	LEAD
Modeling & simulation of acoustic propagation through the atmosphere and seismic propagation through the ground	LEAD
Acoustic experimentation studies	LEAD
Atmospheric effects on transmission	COLLABORATE
Color & other spectral signatures of targets & backgrounds	COLLABORATE
Spatiotemporal characteristics of moving objects in video	LEAD
Relationship Discovery/Pattern of Life Recognition/Anomaly Detection	WATCH
Identification of chemical & biological objects	COLLABORATE

Sensing focuses on the understanding of sensing capabilities and provides the foundation for the effective exploitation of all types of data and information. Researchers in this area maintain an understanding of the sensed phenomena, the effects of the environment on the phenomena, and the transfer functions of the transducers which produce the data. Research in this area does not focus on the actual transducers themselves. Resulting insights help define new or improved algorithms and transducers to provide the data. Work includes Advanced algorithms to improve signal to noise ratios for all sensing modalities.

Passive Electromagnetic Sensing research focuses on the understanding of the detection, classification and identification of passive electromagnetic signatures from intentional and unintentional emissions from electronic and mechanical devices. The goal is to enable exploitation of these signatures for target location and identification.
(i) Passive RF receivers for sensing and exploitation of low signature electronic targets

focuses on very sensitive RF receiver technology to enable detection of low emission targets such as radios, cell phones and other low power electronic equipment.

(ii) Exploitation of unique E&B sensors & algorithms to provide orthogonal data for fusion includes identification of exploitable signatures, association with events or activities of interest, modeling and simulation, multi-modal sensor fusion, and hyper-dimensional signal processing as applied to electric and magnetic fields which are independent in the low frequency, quasi-static regime.

Radar Sensing research focuses on the understanding of the detection, classification and identification of reflected electromagnetic signatures from reflected off of objects. The goal is to enable exploitation of these signatures for target location and identification

(i) Wideband frequency-agile RADAR sensing investigates radar architectures for imaging radar applications including ground penetrating radar, foliage penetrating radar and through the wall radar.

(ii) Advanced algorithms to improve signal to noise ratios develops methods for exploiting sensor and waveform diversity.

Mechanical Wave Sensing research focuses on the understanding of the detection, localization and classification of passive mechanical wave signatures from devices which emit them. The goal is to enable exploitation of these signatures for target location and identification.

(i) Acoustic detection, localization and classification algorithms for acoustic events in diverse acoustic environments. A specific area of focus is persistent detection in urban and cluttered environments.

(ii) Acoustic processing algorithms for transient events from ground and elevated platforms that take into account sound propagation effects.

(iii) Acoustic sensing and processing algorithms on moving platform for enhance situation awareness. Specific areas of focus are reduction of platform and flow noise reduction to increase the effective range.

(iv) Seismic detection and classification of activities in space and time for characterizing humans, vehicles, explosive events, and digging.

(v) Seismic sensing and processing algorithms using distributed arrays of sensors for long range detection and localization of large transient events.

Optical & Photonic Sensing research focuses on the understanding of passive and active optical emissions. The goal is to enable exploitation of these signatures for target location and identification as well as activity determination.

(i) Image and video sampling and reconstruction research focuses on algorithms to provide accurate, lossless reconstruction or enhancement of images while minimizing the numbers of samples used.

(ii) Full motion video processing algorithms for object tracking.

(iii) EO/IR image processing techniques to enhance signal to noise ratios. The focus is on post processing methods to enable improved detection of objects and events.

(iv) EO/IR image spectral processing techniques to extract target signatures from multi-spectral and hyper-spectral images.

(v) Chemical & biological sensing involves acquisition and exploitation of scattered or transmitted signatures of chemical or biological agents in one or more wavelengths of optical radiation ranging from the infrared to the ultraviolet.

Weather and Environmental Sensing research focuses on novel methods, instruments and sensing strategies for efficient and optimal capture of multiple parameters related to prediction and evaluation

(i) Sensors to assist with continuous provision of ground truth to support fine scale weather predictions is concerned with enabling data assimilation into nowcast and forecast models that provide very short term and localized predictions.

(ii) Detection of hazardous chemical & biological aerosols deals with techniques, such as Raman lidar scattering, for optical interrogation of bulk or individual aerosol particles and matching the returns to signatures of hazardous aerosols.

INFORMATION SCIENCES CAMPAIGN's Sensing S&T Footprint	
S&T AREA	**POSTURE**
Sensors to assist with continuous provision of ground truth to support fine scale predictions	COLLABORATE
Passive RF receivers for sensing and exploitation of low signature electronic targets	LEAD
Wideband frequency-agile RADAR sensing	LEAD
Advanced algorithms to improve signal to noise ratios for all sensing modalities	COLLABORATE
Exploitation of unique E&B sensors & algorithms to provide orthogonal data for fusion	LEAD
Robust classification algorithms in diverse acoustic propagation channels	COLLABORATE
Robust detection and localization algorithms (including atmospheric effects) for acoustic signals	LEAD
Sensor and array techniques to enhance signal to noise ratios	COLLABORATE
Image & video sampling and reconstruction algorithms	LEAD
Full Motion video processing algorithms	COLLABORATE
EO/IR image processing techniques to enhance signal to noise	COLLABORATE
Detection of hazardous chemical & biological aerosols	COLLABORATE
Sensors to assist with continuous provision of ground truth to support fine scale weather predictions	COLLABORATE
EO/IR image spectral processing techniques	COLLABORATE

Effecting focuses on the understanding of transforming information into physical events. Research is this area provides insights into the nature and characteristics of related phenomenology, thereby helping design effectors that provide the desired physical effects – motion of a weapon or, electromagnetic influence on an adversary's system, or a desired piece of data to be injected into an adversary's information stream – based on the information provided to the effectors, under the specified, often extreme and austere conditions. The research also provides understanding of the nature and quality of the information that is needed to produce the desired effects.

EM effects research focuses on the coupling of electromagnetic energy signals into electronic devices to create desired effects.

(i) Cognitive radars and smart waveforms for agile transmitters focuses on spectrum sensing approaches to probe the EM RF environment in order to optimize frequency characteristics of radar transmit waveforms to minimize interference and enhance signal to noise ratios.

(ii) New Electronic Warfare concepts research focuses on previously unexploited techniques to exploit coupled energy RF energy in electronic devices to create desired effects.

Social effects research focuses on the social interactions (including human-to-machine interactions) and employment of information to be transformed to create desired effects on humans.

(i) Social sentiment analysis of disparate data sources to extract relevant data/information for information processing, exploitation and dissemination.

(ii) Trust and influence modeling to develop predictive models of social-cognitive aspects multi-genre networks and enhance human performance.

INFORMATION SCIENCES CAMPAIGN's Effecting S&T Footprint	
S&T AREA	**POSTURE**
Cognitive radars and smart waveforms for agile transmitters	LEAD
New EW Concepts	COLLABORATE
Sentiment Analysis	WATCH
Trust and Influence Modeling	WATCH

Data and Information Representation & Management is focused on developing efficient methodologies and techniques to effectively represent, store, and manage sensed data in local caches with minimal space, weight and power requirements; and methodologies for efficient management of information distributed over networks at non-contiguous locations. The goal of this effort is to develop methodologies which aid in the representation of data to the Soldier.

Data representation work focuses on development of data frameworks and efficient schema to enable the gathering, codification and storage of multi-modal sensor data for fusion and data analytics research.

Quality of Data focuses on the intrinsic value and qualities of the data.

INFORMATION SCIENCES CAMPAIGN's Data and Information Representation & Management S&T Footprint	
S&T AREA	**POSTURE**
Data representation	COLLABORATE
Quality of Data	COLLABORATE

SYSTEM INTELLIGENCE & INTELLIGENT SYSTEMS concentrates on understanding and exploiting interactions between information and intelligent systems, such as software agents or robots. Information can be thought of as data in context. In order to fully exploit that data, the context must be taken into account. The data can then be used in providing automated intelligence: perception, reasoning, planning, collaborating, and decision-making. These broad issues in automated intelligence can be applied to a wide range of systems and environments, like cyber virtual environments or decision support. Aspects of Intelligent Systems complement research conducted in the Sciences for Maneuver Campaign, which focuses on Intelligent Systems concepts applied to vehicles or robotic platforms.

Information Understanding addresses critical principles and techniques for processing, extracting and combining data from widely heterogeneous information sources. The overall goal is to transform the information to levels of abstraction that are either more computationally tractable or more useful to the Soldier or both.

Natural Language Processing establishes innovative concepts for rendering the content of large scale text and speech information sources, including foreign language sources, more readily understandable for the Soldier.

(i) Multilingual Computing for Low-Resource Languages draws on novel machine learning techniques to instantiate foreign language translation engines for languages that are not considered commercially viable but that are of critical interest to the Army. The techniques rely heavily on establishing data sets tailored specifically to Army domains.

(ii) Discovery & Extraction of Information from Large Document Caches explores data mining and analytics techniques for rapid access to critical elements of large-scale data sets. Efforts focus on document summarization, author identification, sentiment analysis, concept extraction, and relationship discovery.

(iii) Social Media Exploitation examines the impact of variations in Social Media content on current analytical techniques and the trade-off between increased volume and increased noise. This initiative also examines the extraction of implicit social meaning.

Image Understanding establishes innovative concepts for rendering the content of large scale imagery and video information sources more readily understandable for the Soldier and for computer vision applications.

(i) Object Detection and Recognition research explores algorithms and representational paradigms for automated detection, classification, identification and recognition of physical objects of interest using a range of modalities (EO/IR, radar, ladar, hyper-spectral); and using still images and video. The research overcomes such challenges as cluttered environments, partial occlusion, camouflage and active deception by the adversary.

(ii) Recognition and Classification of Activity explores novel approaches to detecting and identifying activities and events from single or multiple parallel data sets. It includes physical models, behavioral models, processing complexity, and robustness of results.

(iii) Video Summarization research aims at automated methods for transforming a potentially very long video into a few salient elements, such as selected frames, or textual annotation, that convey the key meaning of the video relevant to the Soldier's needs.

(iv) Scene Understanding and Perception research seeks methods to develop higher level of modeling a world from a given set of observations of a complex scene. The resulting model should be readily conveyed to and comprehended by users (human or agents), expressed in a formal representation and consistent with cognitive requirements of the user. The process of forming the model should reflect significant relations between the objects in the scene, infer missing elements of the world representation, and anticipate future events within the world.

INFORMATION SCIENCES CAMPAIGN's Information Understanding S&T Footprint	
S&T AREA	**POSTURE**
Multilingual Computing for Low-Resource Languages	LEAD
Discovery & Extraction of Info from Large Document Caches	COLLABORATE
Social Media Exploitation	COLLABORATE
Object Recognition	COLLABORATE
Recognition and Classification of Activity	COLLABORATE

Video Summarization	COLLABORATE
Scene Understanding	COLLABORATE

Information Fusion establishes advanced theoretical approaches and techniques for integrating data from widely varied physics-based and human sensors, using contextual and semantic information to provide actionable intelligence for the Soldier This research is highly reliant on ongoing projects in trust, quality and value of information, as outlined in the section on Information Management.

Multi-Sensor Information Fusion develops fundamental principles and techniques for integrating and extracting information from multiple sensors of the same type in order to increase the accuracy of single sensor detection, recognition & classification processes.

(i) Multi-Sensor Fusion of EO/IR Videos looks for algorithms that enable fusion of video information produced by a set of sensors. Research challenges include enabling a wider area of coverage, establishing correspondence between objects observed at different locations at different time points, novel registration and correlation methods, and performing modeling and inference over the geometric properties of the scene and objects as sensors see them from different angles.

(ii) Multi-Sensor Fusion of Acoustic Signals aims at fusion of information arriving from multiple acoustic sensors, where the information is produced by such events as aircraft flight, gunfire, mortar and rocket launches. Goals and challenges include improved geolocation and more accurate event detection, use of infrasound for longer range detection, addressing propagation effects, impact of wind noise on detection range and angular accuracy. Use of vector sensors is one approach for potential advances in this area.

(iii) Multi-Sensor Fusion of Passive RF Information seeks novel approaches to enhancing accuracy of detection, tracking, signature recognition, and geo-location of objects that emit RF signals, using an array of passive RF sensors. Such approaches must deal with very weak RF signals, differential propagation losses, and much cluttered RF environment.

Heterogeneous-Sensor Information Fusion establishes innovative concepts and methods for providing actionable intelligence to Soldiers based on information obtained from widely heterogeneous sources. Leveraging such concepts as cross-training and reasoning under uncertainty, these efforts seek to provide reliable real-time semantic descriptions and summaries of objects to avoid information overload.

(i) Context-Aware Collection for Fusion of Heterogeneous Information focuses on automated control of assets to collect mission critical data elements in urban environments in a manner suitable for effective fusion of heterogeneous information to enable effective operations.

(ii) Mission-Adaptive Collection research explores the use of mission context, Quality-of-Information and Value-of-Information to inform and direct data collection based on integrated mission and C2 requirements as well as network state. The goal is to shape, filter, prioritize and refine information provided through tactical ISR products.

(iii) Integrated Text and Video Analytics seeks cross-cutting text and video analytics concepts for providing stronger hierarchical structures for imagery and video, enabling cross training of analytical techniques between heterogeneous media, and sharing context across media when parallel text and video are available.

(iv) Fusion of Passive RF, EO/IR and Acoustic research focuses on approaches to inte-

grating information resulting from highly dissimilar physical phenomenology to enhance accuracy and suppress false alarm in detection and tracking of targets that are difficult to observe by any single modality.

INFORMATION SCIENCES CAMPAIGN's Information Fusion S&T Footprint	
S&T AREA	**POSTURE**
Multi-Sensor Fusion of EO/IR Videos	COLLABORATE
Multi-Sensor Fusion of Acoustic Signals	COLLABORATE
Multi-Sensor Fusion of Passive RF Information	LEAD
Context-Aware Collection/Fusion of Heterogeneous Information	COLLABORATE
Mission-Adaptive Collection	COLLABORATE
Integrated Text and Video Analytics	COLLABORATE
Fusion of Passive RF, EO/IR and Acoustic	LEAD

Computational Intelligence seeks computationally feasible techniques and theories to address the synergistic integration of components of intelligent behavior, including perception, reasoning, planning/execution, and decision making. These behaviors can be individual or collaborative. The overall objective is to provide computational methods to support, or in some way augment, the Soldier in accomplishing tactical missions.

Perception and Cognition establishes innovative concepts for recognizing and understanding the world in which the system's intelligent agents operate.

(i) Cognitive Modeling draws from the fields of neuroscience and neural networks to provide a framework for representing, maintaining and computing across complex components of behaviors of intelligent agents.

(ii) Pattern Recognition and Mapping in Military Environments addresses the critical components of individually or collaboratively mapping newly encountered abstract or physical spaces. This research incorporates different time and spatial scales and addresses robust operation in complex and dynamic environments, uncertainty, and fusion of heterogeneous information sources. While related commercial activities pertain to structured environments (roads and buildings) the Army requires recognition and mapping tools applicable to unstructured and challenging environments.

Computational Reasoning addresses the fundamental mathematics of machine learning, pattern recognition, reasoning under uncertainty and prediction. While expertise is critical to intelligence research, key advances are largely leveraged from academia.

Planning and Execution addresses methodologies and techniques to effectively assess an operational environment then employ intelligence technologies during Soldier training, tactical mission planning, and ultimately tactical mission execution. Assessments of risk and prediction of outcome are difficult to model and often rely on probabilistic approaches characterizing outcome likelihoods.

(i) Weather Forecasts in Tactical Environments focuses on novel methods for localized atmospheric sensing, boundary layer modeling, and micro-scale atmospheric modeling, to produce highly accurate near-term forecasts of weather effects on military operations.

(ii) Intelligent Control of Tactical Mission Execution focuses on techniques to exploit intelligent systems to assess and manage military-relevant activities in real-time. This thrust requires tight coupling among efforts across the Information Sciences Campaign, as

sensing, intelligence, communications and user interface are all critical component.

(iii) Estimates of Adversarial Dynamics couples disparate sources of data and information and builds predictive adversarial behavior models that reason about intent.

(iv) Forecasting Social and Political Activity addresses predictive models that expand the concept of environmental forecasts to such conditions as availability of power or food sources or potential for social unrest or insurgency activity. As military operations continue to evolve, these capabilities will be of greater and greater concern.

Decision Making addresses cross-cutting fundamental principles of decision science, neuroscience and mathematics to enable timely near-optimal decision making in dynamic, uncertain, and complex tactical environments. In well-constrained situations, software agents emulate decision makers. Robotics pushes that process even further as more complex missions and environments are supported. Given the state of the art in automated intelligence, many decisions will remain in the hands of the user. This research also addresses techniques for supporting a human-in-the-loop in making the tradeoff analysis required to fully consider a series of related forecasts and potential courses of action. Work is closely aligned with the Collaboration and Negotiation outlined in later pages.

(i) Collaborative Task and Resource Allocation enables real-time distribution of limited resources in austere, dynamic environments. Its focus is on long-duration missions.

(ii) Distributed and Decentralized Decision Making explores novel techniques for collaborative mission planning and execution with limited inter-agent interactions to overcome limited infrastructure constraints.

(iii) Military Course of Action Analysis for Decision Support provides concepts for predicting and choosing among a series of military outcomes. It addresses evolving constraints as well as the impact of trust/quality/value of information.

(iv) Decision Making in Coalition Operations explores the impact of conflicting constraints and priorities among partner decision makers on rank ordering algorithms.

INFORMATION SCIENCES CAMPAIGN's Computational Intelligence S&T Footprint	
S&T AREA	**POSTURE**
Cognitive Modeling	COLLABORATE
Pattern Recognition & Mapping in Military Environments	COLLABORATE
Computational Reasoning	WATCH
Weather Forecasts	LEAD
Intelligent Control of Tactical Mission Execution	COLLABORATE
Estimates of Adversarial Dynamics	COLLABORATE
Forecasting Social and Political Activity	WATCH
Collaborative Task and Resource Allocation	COLLABORATE
Distributed and Decentralized Decision Making	COLLABORATE
Military Course of Action Analysis for Decision Support	WATCH
Decision Making in Coalition Operations	COLLABORATE

HUMAN & INFORMATION INTERACTION research concentrates on understanding and exploiting interactions between information and humans. It involves complex mixed-initiative processes of information acquisition, processing and comprehension. Aspects of this research complement efforts in the Human Sciences Campaign, with the delineation being that research in the Information Sciences Campaign places greater emphasis on information structure, dynamics, phenomena and properties.

Information Access research addresses human-in-the-loop strategies for rapid exploitation of massive data sets. These information sources are assumed to be heterogeneous, widely distributed, and used for real-time analytics to support tactical operations.

Adaptive Retrieval establishes innovative concepts for ranking, filtering, and highlighting information specifically sought out by the user.

(i) Decision Driven Retrieval draws on intelligent systems technology to tailor the collection of information to mission-relevant events.

(ii) Scalable Feedback Mechanisms explores policy based information exchange techniques to adapt the flow of information to a mix of available resources.

Information Discovery seeks to advance theoretical approaches for identifying critical data of which the user is unaware. It leverages knowledge of such concepts as the user's mission, interests, and capabilities, as well as an understanding of the operating environment to, to recognize anomalies, trends, or high value data on behalf of the user.

(i) Big Data Mining explores the use of reach-back or Cloud concepts to leverage High Performance Computing, providing real-time data mining techniques for trend analysis and anomaly detection in tactical environments.

(ii) Recommender Research draws on machine learning techniques to instantiate user profiles enabling users to rapidly learn about critical data sources from each other.

Human-Machine Discourse addresses concepts for establishing effective methods for providing a more natural interaction between humans and machines.

(i) Cognition Driven Discovery establishes concepts for addressing information access as a means of "filling in the blanks" on behalf of the user to support decision making.

(ii) Natural Language Interaction focuses on use of natural language to express the components of a world model associated with the system domain. The goal is to have a natural-language human-machine interface that is computationally tractable.

INFORMATION SCIENCES CAMPAIGN's Information Access S&T Footprint	
S&T AREA	**POSTURE**
Decision Driven Retrieval	COLLABORATE
Scalable Feedback Mechanisms	COLLABORATE
Big Data Mining	COLLABORATE
Recommender Research	WATCH
Cognition Driven Discovery	COLLABORATE
Natural Language Interaction	COLLABORATE

Collaboration and Negotiation seeks theories and techniques for better understanding and supporting one-to-one, one-to-many, and many-to-many interactions supporting joint decision making between and among humans and machines.

Human-Machine Interaction research addresses techniques for distributing a shared task among multiple team members in a manner that optimizes overall performance.

(i) Human-System Socio-Cybernetics seeks to define the social processes that impact communication and control in human-machine interaction.

(ii) Collaborative and Teaming Systems provides cross-cutting research in Social Science and Computer Science to advance understanding of human-machine interaction to optimize integrated system performance. The focus of this research in on effective strategies for distributing intelligent behaviors (perception, reasoning, planning and decision making) to enhance mission outcome.

(iii) Impacts of Trust and Value of Information on Collaboration and Negotiation explores the impact of trust on decision making and its effect on overall integrated (human-machine) performance.

(iv) Cognition-Aware Presentation of Tactical Information explores the use and integration of a variety of wearable physiological sensors to determine the user's physiological and cognitive state and adapt the presentation and dissemination of tactical information accordingly.

Distributed Human-Human Interaction research is focused on cross cutting social science, communications science, and computer science concepts with a focus on advancing our ability to collaborate and solve problems in distributed, complex networked environments.

(i) Trust Dynamics in Distributed Information Systems explores the impact of distributed interaction technology on the trust dynamic between and among users.

(ii) Distributed Problem Solving examines the impact of distributed technology on consensus building, decision quality, and decision timeliness. The use of distributed systems and social media show promise of new concepts for problem solving using human parallel processors in the mix. The goal of this research is to address the strengths and weakness of this concept.

INFORMATION SCIENCES CAMPAIGN's Collaboration and Negotiation S&T Footprint	
S&T AREA	**POSTURE**
Human-Systems Socio-Cybernetics	COLLABORATE
Collaboration and Teaming Systems	COLLABORATE
Impacts of Trust and Value on Collaboration & Negotiation	COLLABORATE
Cognition-Aware Presentation of Tactical Information	COLLABORATE
Trust Dynamics in Distributed Information Systems	COLLABORATE
Distributed Problem Solving	COLLABORATE

NETWORKS AND COMMUNICATIONS research concentrates on understanding and exploiting information's interactions with socio-technical networks, particularly communications, and command and control networks, both formal and social. Of particular importance is Network Science – the study of structure, dynamics, behaviors and evolutions of networks, especially in the context of interactions between communications, information and social networks.

Channels and Protocols research deals with means to transfer information between nodes of the network and through the network to the right destination in an efficient and robust manner. This broad area includes media through which a message is sent, the phenomenology of sending the message, the encoding and decoding means, the properties of the channel. It also includes formats, rules and algorithms that govern how the information moves through the network.

Unconventional Communication Networks research is focused on the study and capability development of unconventional alternative networks to provide needed network diversity, robustness, and survivability. While traditional military radio communications are limited in bandwidth and channel allocation, commercial wireless communication networks have embraced multi-standard heterogeneous approaches that have greatly increased the quality and types of mobile, wireless information delivery. Inspired by this success, the Information Sciences Campaign is exploring new heterogeneous approaches to encoding, transmitting, deconflicting and optimizing information delivery through previously unexplored networks configurations, channels, protocols and allocation techniques. This effort is dedicated to better understanding the dynamics; useful properties; capacities and limits of alternative communication networks; hybrid methods of information delivery with persistent information services in challenging terrain, under challenging atmospheric conditions, and under sophisticated adversarial disruptions.

(i) Information-Carrying Capacities of RF and non-RF Networks research studies rigorous models that enable characterization and prediction of the amount of information that a network can carry to the Soldiers in harsh environments of the Army battlefield. This research in particular seeks opportunities in underutilized parts of the RF spectrum as well as in non-RF channels that are likely to be less vulnerable to disruption.

(ii) Heterogeneous Hybrid Networking research focuses on methods, models and properties of networks that combine several types of channels, diverse protocols, and dissimilar nature of the communication nodes. Properties of network survivability and security can be enhanced by such heterogeneity.

(iii) Quantum Networking research explores techniques, architectures, protocols, models and properties pertaining to networks that take advantage of quantum and related effects for teleportation and other modes of transmitting information on the battlefield.

(iv) Consumer Communication Networks and Cellular Communications research follows ongoing, rapidly evolving advances in consumer networks, especially mobile communications as instructive examples of opportunities potentially applicable to the Army needs.

Adaptive Protocols research is focused on developing understanding, methodologies, and techniques pertaining to network protocols, especially those for highly heterogeneous networks – incorporating multi-wavelengths, autonomous air and ground nodes, and providing service to a variety of systems from dismounts to large platforms. Adaptive protocols are expected to provide a software paradigm to enhance network cognition and provide information when and where it is needed. Research challenges include distributed operation, robustness, provability, and decomposition.

(i) Very Low-Power Protocols for Sensor Radio Networks research focuses on highly demanding problem of enabling long-time operation of networked unattended ground sensors where battery life is paramount and protocols must minimize power consumption in a way that supports dynamically changing requirements of the network.

(ii) IP and Cellular Protocols research follows and adapts where appropriate the developments that take place primarily outside of Army research, but which can be a fertile source of innovations for Army communications protocol.

INFORMATION SCIENCES CAMPAIGN's Channel and Protocols S&T Footprint	
S&T AREA	**POSTURE**
Information-carrying Capacities of RF and non-RF networks	COLLABORATE
Heterogeneous Hybrid Networking	COLLABORATE
Quantum Networking	COLLABORATE
Consumer Communication Networks and Cellular Communications	WATCH
Very Low-Power Protocols for Sensors Radio Networks	LEAD
IP and Cellular Protocols	WATCH

Control and Behavior research focuses on the complex dynamic behaviors – and the approaches to controlling such behaviors – that emerges in interaction and co-evolution of networks that include command, information, social, and physical networks, and may also span coalition partnerships. While a significant body of research now exists for static networks and internets, dynamics and co-evolution present significant challenges to modeling and understanding. Enhanced understanding will aid with the Adaptive Protocols and Self-adaptive Networks research areas.

Assessment of Behavior research area is dedicated to developing understanding, methodologies, and techniques to enable tools for the analysis of difficult to monitor networks. Knowledge gained through these efforts is expected to have a significant impact on Army's capability to assess and manage mobile, rapidly changing, distributed, coalition network state. Tools developed as a result of these efforts are also expected to enable the Army of the future to analyze adversarial networks to infer social or command hierarchy from sparse message collection.

(i) Modeling & Analysis of Groups in Multi-genre Networks seek expressive mathematical models for multi-genre networks of groups and evolving group phenomena, focusing on group relationships to understand complex group dynamics that span multiple genres – such as information and social networks.

(ii) Discovering Network Processes in Time-evolving Networks research focuses on developing mathematical foundations for the discovery of significant network processes in time-varying multi-genre networks. This will lead to improved understanding of fundamental properties of dynamic multi-genre networks. Success in this research may lead to new approaches to monitoring and managing friendly communications networks.

Control of Behavior research is dedicated to developing understanding, methodologies, and techniques leading to realization of intelligent, mission-tailorable, and reconfigurable networks for rapid network reconfiguration, mission re-tasking, and healing. Control or even influencing is particularly challenged in complex interactions of social, information and communication networks. Underpinned by adaptive protocols, network reconfiguration may include physical change as well as information transfer redirection to optimize performance based on operational needs and environmental conditions.

(i) Designing & Controlling Composite Networks research focuses on mathematical foundations for controlling dynamic multi-genre networks – such as the Army command, control and communications networks -- by optimally modifying network structure & attributes to allow desirable multi-genre network properties to be created & sustained over time without violating constraints.

(ii) Controllability in Complex Networks research studies the means by which – and the limits to which -- a network can be controlled given its structure, inherent properties, exigent factors and objectives. This involves mathematically-grounded techniques to control complex networks of different types (temporal, layered, co-evolving, and nonlinear) and spanning multiple genres.

(iii) Network Self-Control and Adaptation under the Conditions of High Mobility explores unique constraints and means to overcome them as pertains to control and self-control of networks that rapidly change, particularly due to high mobility over a terrain that impact connectivity of the network.

INFORMATION SCIENCES CAMPAIGN's Control and Behavior S&T Footprint	
S&T AREA	**POSTURE**
Modeling & Analysis of Groups in Multi-genre Net	COLLABORATE
Discovering Network Processes in Time-evolving Networks	COLLABORATE
Designing & Controlling Composite Network	COLLABORATE
Controllability in Complex Network	COLLABORATE
Network Self-control and Adaptation under the Conditions of High Mobility	LEAD

Information Delivery research involves study of methods, theories, models and properties pertaining to storage, management, transformations, transmission and delivery of information – mission-relevant and context-appropriate – within and through the socio-technical networks, in such a manner that the information needs of the Soldiers are met to the maximum possible degree at the right place and at the right time, in spite of environmental and adversarial disruptions. The dynamics of information delivery is dependent on complex interactions of information, social and communications networks.

Network-based Information Processing involves storage, retrieval, caching, duplicating, compressing, fusing and other transformations that utilize communication networks and processing nodes, and also create and continually modify the distributed networks of information.

(i) Constructing Unified, Structured Knowledge Networks research aims at reliable information network construction through progressive source processing and network refinement, linking entities, and understanding human behavior. The resulting networked collections of knowledge should be context-aware and mission aware, and yet be readily distributed over heterogeneous networks and adaptable to diverse needs.

(ii) Quality-aware Semantic Video Analytics research focuses on massive and rapidly growing information resources on the battlefield – video. The results of this research will lead to network-distributed video analytics to enable quality-aware semantic querying and searching of videos to retrieve relevant information from various networked locations while adapting in-situ to dynamically varying resources of the network.

(iii) Distributed, User-oriented Multi-scale Network Summarization and Online Analytical Processing research explores approaches to distributed, multi-scale, multi-genre information network summarization, online analytical processing, and situation analysis to support online information processing for diverse groups of users.

Context-sensitive Distribution research studies means by which information can be delivered to the users in a way that maximizes its utility to the user while avoiding excessive volume of transmissions with associated time delays and resource consumption. This involves approaches to characterizing the content and properties of the information and aligning it with needs of the user.

(i) Semantic Information Theory seeks foundations for the characterization and encoding of information with primary focus on the semantics of what is being communicated. It considers shared knowledge of sender and receiver so that less information, more densely coded can be delivered over noisy channels, to improve fundamental limits of communications.

(ii) Semantic Quality-aware Information Delivery research aims at the goal of delivering to Soldiers the information with content that matches their decision-making needs. To this

end, it investigates approaches to jointly considering semantic reasoning (inferencing), relationships between entities and information, and tactical network characteristics to maximize semantic information delivery.

(iii) Information-based Decision Making & Trust in Networks research area focuses on ways to identify factors and methods for enhancing human's and agent's trust in information and for enhancing distributed decision-making in networked environments given varying levels of the available information quality and quantity, and degrees of automation.

INFORMATION SCIENCES CAMPAIGN's Information Delivery S&T Footprint	
S&T AREA	**POSTURE**
Contructing Unified, Structured Knowledge Networks	
Quality-aware Semantic Video Analytics	COLLABORATE
Distributed, User-oriented Multi-scale Network Summarization & Online Processing	COLLABORATE
Semantic Information Theory	COLLABORATE
Semantic Quality-aware Information Delivery	COLLABORATE
Information-based Decision Making & Trust in Networks	LEAD

CYBER SECURITY research concentrates on understanding and exploiting interactions of information with cyber attackers – human and/or intelligent agents. These interactions involve friendly operations against adversary information systems and networks, defense of friendly information systems and networks, and assurance of persistent information support to Soldiers even when parts of the friendly systems and networks are compromised.

Threat Defeat research in cyber security seeks to develop theories and models that relate properties and capabilities of cyber threat detection, recognition and defeat processes/mechanisms to properties of a malicious activity, and of properties of Army networks. This research informs development of approaches to rapid adaptation of a detection and prevention technique or algorithm as new threats emerge. The focus is on both detection and defeat of highly sophisticated, stealthy attackers that employ techniques unlike those of more conventional financially-oriented threats addressed by industry; in addition the focus is on techniques relevant to Army-specific convergent networks that combine strategic and tactical elements, each with their own set of unique challenges.

Understanding the Cyber Threat research focuses on approaches, models and algorithms that provide underpin on developing a detailed understanding of cyber attackers, their tools, techniques, tactics and procedures, infrastructure, and psychosocial aspects of the intent and preferences of their actions. Knowledge gained through this effort is expected to lead to methodologies and techniques to triage relevant data embedded within large volumes of benign artifacts; and counter an attacker's active efforts to conceal and disguise its tools and techniques. In an Army context, such learning and analyses are challenged by the large attack surface of both the adversary and friendly network. Results of these assessments are expected to be relevant to both defensive and offensive operations.

(i) Analyzing Adversary's Infrastructure explores means to learn and infer information about the structure, dynamics, and properties of adversary networks. Such activities must be stealthy in order to minimize the scope of the adversary's knowledge; and mindful of adversary efforts at concealment and deception.

(ii) Inference of Attacker TTPs focuses on understanding of the adversary's tactics, tech-

niques and procedures while constrained by limited observability and often well-disguised nature of the available information regarding the adversary's activities on the friendly networks. Approaches to creating computational architectures and algorithms are important here as well.

(iii)Psychosocial Aspects of Adversary Actions are important topics of study for the purposes of anticipating the likely next action of the adversary; for creating models of adversary attacks and other malicious activities; and for crafting techniques of defeating the adversarial actions.

Automated Detection of Hostile Activities pursues greater understanding, including theories, models, and optimized methods, of properties and behaviors of processes by which automated and human agents detect, recognize and comprehend malicious activities conducted of adversaries on friendly networks and hosts.

(i) Algorithms of Automated Learning for Detection are focused on novel algorithmic approaches to automated learning, detection, recognition and analysis of malicious activities. Particularly promising are approaches that use unsupervised learning, or very limited supervision, of anomalous and potentially malicious low-observable events.

(ii) Cognitive Effects in Cyber Analysis research is focused on psychosocial and cognitive effects and approaches to optimizing the performance of human cyber analysts. Since teams of human defenders are the key link in such analyses, a theoretical understanding of the socio-linguistic and socio-cognitive factors that impact the decision making of the user/Soldier, defender/analyst, and adversary is needed.

Prevention and Defeat of Hostile Activities explores a broad range of means by which cyber defenders of friendly networks can either prevent a hostile activities from being initiated on the friendly networks, or to defeat it effectively and rapidly after it has been detected, with minimal disruptions to the operations and missions supported by the network.

(i) Denial and Disruption efforts are focused on novel approaches to using denial, disruption, and deception against attacker's tactics and techniques. The research challenges in this direction include the need for theoretically-grounded models of states and properties of such denial activities, and their probability of success as a function of properties of the network and threats.

(ii) Financial Fraud Prevention investigates rapidly evolving advances in financial fraud detection and prevention as an instructive example of defense against sophisticated threat. Borrowing ideas and insights from the large and well-funded financial cyber security industry has been a valuable way to fertilize cyber research relevant to the needs of the Army.

INFORMATION SCIENCES CAMPAIGN's Threat Defeat S&T Footprint	
S&T AREA	**POSTURE**
Analyzing Adversary's Infrastructure	COLLABORATE
Inference of Attacker TTPs	LEAD
Psychosocial Aspects of Adversary action	COLLABORATE
Algorithms of Automated Learning for Detection	LEAD
Cognitive Effects in Cyber Analysis	COLLABORATE
Denial and Disruption	COLLABORATE
Financial Fraud Prevention	WATCH

Resilience research studies the means by which a network of computing and communicating devices can be protected, managed and operated in a way that minimizes the risk to –and the extent of -- its disruption or degradation while ensuring that the network is able to recover as rapidly and as fully as practical.

Risk Characterization research seeks to develop theories and models that relate fundamental properties and features of dynamic risk assessment algorithms to the fundamental properties of dynamic cyber threats, the Army's networks, and defensive mechanisms. This research also explores approaches to identification of system and network vulnerabilities and rapid recognition of means through which these vulnerabilities can be exploited. While much of the current practice in these areas depends on highly tailored, one-of-a-kind discoveries and artisan tool development, the intent of the research is to develop fundamental knowledge that would lead to systematic means for vulnerability discovery, and potential exploit identification. Research in this area are expected to lead to theoretically-grounded techniques and tools to synthesize, modify, adapt, or redesign algorithms that reliably compute risks imposed by new cyber threats to Army networks and changes to networks to mitigate such threats.

(i) Metrics and algorithms for risk assessment research focuses on theoretical and empirical approaches, metrics and algorithms to assess risk to friendly network from adversary malicious activities. The challenges include complex influences of network topology and functions distribution as well as effects induced by behaviors of users and defenders.

(ii) Risk data collection and fusion research explores architectures and methods for collection and fusion of massive data sets from friendly networks to support risk assessment. Incompleteness, intermittent availability, potential deception, heterogeneity and noisiness of the data are among the technical challenges that this research area will address.

(iii) Assessing vulnerabilities and trustworthiness research studies approaches to assessing vulnerabilities and trustworthiness of systems and networks. Quantifying such attributes in a theoretically grounded manner, and with attention to dynamic nature of vulnerabilities and trust, is critical.

(iv) Anticipating the impacts of malicious activities research aims to develop models and algorithms that support anticipating the nature and extent of impacts on friendly network from malicious activities. The challenges include the need to account for mission-dependency, effects of simultaneous actions of defenders and attackers, and user reactions.

(v) Assessment by Red-Teaming involves research into techniques and tools for effective and comprehensive red-teaming to assess resilience of friendly networks. The goals include rigorous, principled assessments that produce results comparable across a broad range of systems and experiences of human red-team members.

Agile Adaptation research seeks to develop theories and models to support planning and control of a means by which a network or system changes its attributes, configuration, allocation of functions and topology, for the purposes of avoiding, mitigating or repairing the effects of a hostile cyber attack. Knowledge gained through these efforts is expected to provide greater insight into the influences that fundamental threat properties exert on control and end-state of the cyber maneuver.

(i) Methods for rapid continuous changes research studies methods for rapid continuous changes in features of friendly networks, such as IPs, to confuse and degrade adversary intelligence gathering as well as the execution of penetration and further phases of a compromise. Related terms include Cyber Maneuver, Moving Target Defense and Agile Recovery.

(ii) Planning and control of cyber maneuvers research area focuses on models and algorithms for planning and control of cyber maneuvers (changes in network and node config-

urations) to minimize damage due to an ongoing attack. This research touches on many of the traditional issues of planning and research, but with unique complications and constraints of cyber operations.

(iii) Approaches to rapid recovery research explore methods to achieve rapid and substantial recovery of network capability after a major compromise by adversary action. Resilience of the network, the success of ongoing operations supported by the network, and risk of further compromises by the adversary are all dependent on the recovery technique.

INFORMATION SCIENCES CAMPAIGN's Resilience S&T Footprint	
S&T AREA	**POSTURE**
Metrics and algorithms for risk assessment	COLLABORATE
Risk data collection and fusion	LEAD
Assessing vulnerabilities and trustworthiness	COLLABORATE
Anticipating the impacts of malicious activities	COLLABORATE
Assessment by read-teaming	COLLABORATE
Methods for rapid continuous changes	COLLABORATE
Planning and control of cyber maneuvers	COLLABORATE
Approaches to rapid recovery	COLLABORATE

SCIENCES FOR LETHALITY-AND-PROTECTION CAMPAIGN

MISSION: To discover, innovate, and transition S&T capabilities that (1) facilitate the development of discriminant lethality across a broad range of missions; (2) facilitate the development of protection systems that are effective, fieldable, and affordable against a broad array of threats; and (3) enable robust technical tools and methodologies for evaluation and combat decision aids.

VISION: Lethality systems available to commanders of the Army of 2030 are precise, long range, and highly mobile. Protection systems are light weight, low burden, affordable, and resilient towards a broad array of threats. A fundamental understanding of injury mechanisms is exploited for a safer, more effective force. A globally responsive, lethal, and resilient force serves as a significant deterrent to rising conflict. The desired end state is to leverage the range of S&T enablers to provide forces with the right lethality at any place and time without increased warfighter risk and warfighter protection against the continuum of threats without degrading combat power.

SCIENCES FOR LETHALITY-AND-PROTECTION CAMPAIGN PLAN

ARL's S&T investments in Sciences-for-Lethality and Protection are focused on gaining a greater understanding and discovery of mechanisms and on generating concepts and emerging technologies that support lethality and protection systems, and the mechanisms of injury affecting the warfighter. Knowledge and concepts gained through these research efforts will lead to technologies that enable a broad array of discriminate lethality systems as well as resilient protection systems and reduced incidents and severity of combat casualties. Campaign competencies and knowledge can support the Army through 2025, and the new technologies are essential for Lethality and Protection Superiority of the Army of 2030 and beyond.

Fundamental research efforts in the Sciences for Lethality and Protection Campaign are targeted at achieving seven overriding functional goals including
- *Mobile protected fire power for expeditionary forces.*
- *Desired effects at standoff ranges for moving targets in access denied environments.*
- *Soldier protection with zero impact on effectiveness.*
- *Adaptive weapon systems empowering the Soldier/Squad to focus on the fight.*
- *Completely reversible human effects in any situation.*
- *Robust, reliable weapons/platform evaluation at significantly reduced cost.*
- *Robust tools for battle damage assessment and combat decision aids.*

These goals are addressed through research in technology areas – areas that encompass fundamental technology building blocks and scientific advances through which innovation is realized. Combinations of existing and new innovative technologies will be brought together through partnerships to realize disruptive system advances. All of these advances are driven by overcoming key learning and technical challenges required to further enable the Army of 2030 and beyond.

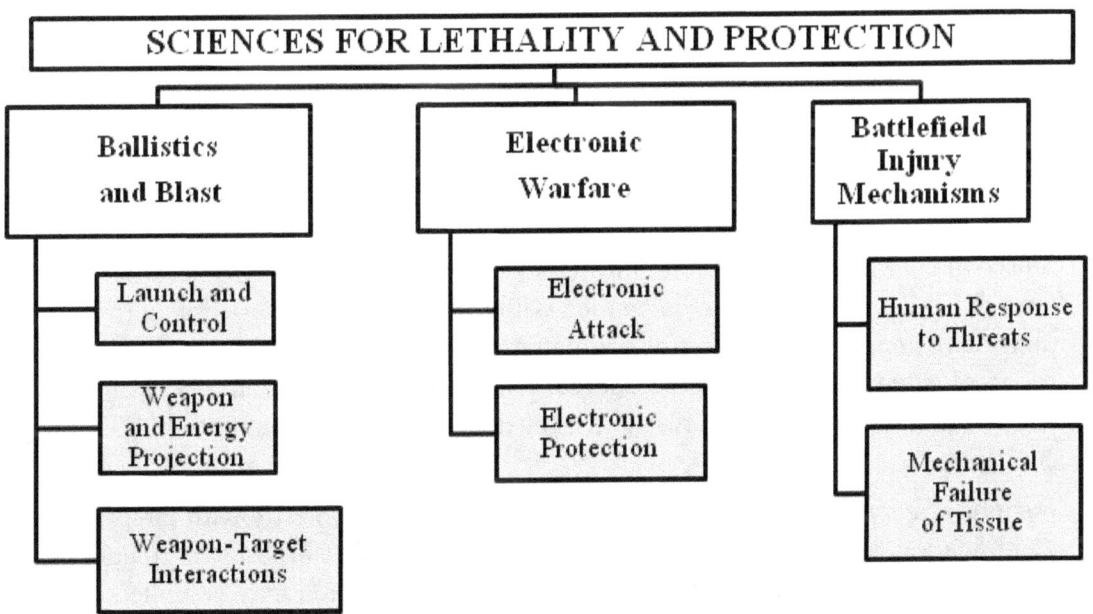

Levels 1 through 3 of the Sciences for Lethality-and-Protection Campaign Plan Taxonomy

BALLISTICS AND BLAST RESEARCH concentrates on understanding and exploiting the fundamental aspects of launch and control; weapons and energy projection; electronic attack/protection; and weapon-target interaction across the spectrum of lethal/non-lethal mechanisms and threats

Launch and Control is focused on fundamental research to support guns and missile launchers and fire control systems. ARL works closely with our partners across the Launch and Control domain.

Guns and Launchers research focuses on improving the performance of systems used to propel and launch munitions. Examples include increasing weapons accuracy, rate of fire, mitigating recoil, and improvements to size, weight, and power while enabling increased range, the study of weapons system dynamics, thermal management, reliability, and erosion.

Technical Fire Control focuses on understanding and conceiving technologies to improve firing and accuracy of weapons systems. Research includes understanding error budgets, weapon and potentially shooter dynamics, and controlling for external factors such as met conditions. Technologies include hardware, software, and algorithms.

SCIENCES FOR LETHALITY AND PROTECTION's Launch and Control S&T Footprint	
S&T AREA	**POSTURE**
Guns and Launchers	COLLABORATE
Technical Fire Control	COLLABORATE

Weapons and Energy Projection is focused on gaining a fundamental understanding of complex flight behaviors – relying on the science of fluid mechanics and rigid body dynamics to enable high maneuverability airframes to intercept moving targets or evade counter measures. Platform maneuverability and navigation technologies for assured delivery of the lethal payload are the primary areas of research interest in this effort.

Maneuverability research is dedicated to developing understanding, methodologies, and techniques to realize highly reliable, throttleable, power energetic, and affordable propulsion components and materials that operate in extreme thermal and physical environments. The goal of this effort is better understand and exploit efficient divert and maneuver mechanisms that may be applied to lethal platforms.

Navigation research focuses on operating lethal platforms in access-denied environments. Algorithms for image-based navigation, to include target acquisition, target tracking, and state estimation, are a primary interest. Research into various low cost sensor modalities such as visible/infrared imagers and micro-electromechanical systems (MEMS) inertial sensors is applied with intelligent signal processing to data and innovative concepts necessary for navigation in stressed environments. Innovations for accelerated, reliable, and efficient real time communication and processing are a consideration throughout this research to enable swarming and parent-child munitions concepts.

Weapons Sensors research focuses on sensors involved primarily with target location, identification, signature measurement, and tracking for the purposes of guidance, timing and fuzing, and potentially model selection. This research may be linked closely with maneuverability and navigation research depending on the class of munitions and target set. Particular challenges include locating and identifying targets in obscured, concealed, or camouflaged environments; fusion of information from disparate sensors; ruggedization; and counter measures and counter-counter measures.

Energetic Materials and Propulsion research focuses on all aspects of improved gun and missile propellant formulations, from synthesis and processing through use and demilitarization; ignition and combustion mechanisms and modeling; charge and igniter design; interior ballistic modeling; signature management; and novel diagnostics. Novel propulsion approaches are explored for leap-ahead efficiency and effectiveness from weapons systems.

SCIENCES FOR LETHALITY AND PROTECTION's Weapons and Energy Projection S&T Footprint	
S&T AREA	POSTURE
Projectile Maneuverability	LEAD
Projectile Navigation	LEAD
Weapon Sensors	LEAD
Energetic Materials and Propulsion	LEAD

Weapon-Target Interactions research is focused on understanding and exploiting broad classes of weapons-target interactions for efficient, effective lethality and protection. These research efforts are expected to provide a spectrum of capabilities from non-lethal technologies, to overwhelming lethality, to active counter-measures, and terminal point defense.

Penetrators and Warheads research efforts are focused on scalable and tailorable technologies; the capability to defeat advanced future threats; and significantly reducing weapon costs and size. Targets of interest include personnel, infrastructure, and mobile enemy platforms.

Munition Response research focuses on understanding and mitigating the likelihood and severity of an unplanned munition reaction to hostile threats and accidental stimuli. Challenges include both raising the threshold stimulus required for the initiation of a reaction as well as lowering the severity of the reaction and consequence of an unplanned event. Improved models are developed and mitigation approaches are explored at the level of the munition as well as at in the storage, shipping and tactical configurations.

Disruptive Energetics research is focused on exploration and maturation of formulations energetic materials which are expected to be critical to the revolutionary advancement of both propulsion and effects on target. Research in this area seeks to understand very high energy density storage and release on desired timescales, methods to balance various parameters in energetic formulations, and prediction of formulation ingredient compatibility. Improved models, concepts, and new energetic materials for propulsion are expected to provide enhance range, speed of engagement, and maneuverability while maintaining weapons safety and surety. Additionally, game-changing energetic concepts with an order of magnitude more potential than conventional energetic are being pursued and are expected to enable new approaches to lethality, particularly when partnered with emerging accuracy and precision advances.

Armor research focuses on the terminal ballistic mechanisms of passive and active materials systems against multiple classes of threats – fragments, kinetic energy projectiles, shape-charge-jets, and other explosively formed penetrators – both from a single and multi-hit perspective. This effort couples fundamental laboratory and fundamental range experiments to gain a robust understanding of mechanical, electromagnetic, and explosive behaviors. Challenges include reduced size, weight, and power along with increased effectiveness for potential future threats.

Soldiers Personal Protection Equipment (PPE) research focuses on developing comparatively thinner, lighter, ballistic protection with reduced physical burden and modularity for the warfighter. Research in this area includes protection for head, body, eye and extremities. Research interests include PPE to defeat both penetrating and blunt trauma threats in a single protective system. A particular challenge is reducing the burden while increasing the ability to defeat advanced threats and providing efficient mission selectable protection.

Hit Avoidance Technologies focuses on mechanisms and concepts to conceal, deceive, or disrupt threat targeting, terminal guidance, weapon sensor, or countermeasure capabilities to avoid being engaged by the threat weapon or countermeasure.

Active, adaptive and collaborative Protection research focuses on concept, mechanism, and models across the potential chain of events leading to effective active defense. Adaptive protection seeks mechanisms and combinations of novel technologies to exploit threat information to strengthen existing protection capability enabling protection levels otherwise not physically possible. Collaborative defense is based on significantly increased efficiencies that are possible by off loading functions for active defense to other platforms or devices. The protection concepts apply across the entire spectrum of threats.

Fuze and S&A research focuses on mechanisms and concepts required for advanced fuzing. Of particular interest are multi-mode fuzing and fuzing hardened for both the launch and threat engagement environment. Additional focus areas include miniaturization and smart fuzing for target identification. Future areas include collateral fuzing and initiation for swarming and combined effects.

Decoys and Obscurants focuses on understanding mechanisms of decoy and obscurant effectiveness and conceiving new decoys, obscurants, and dissemination technologies for the purposes of avoiding detection and engagement by existing and potential threat weapons.

Fire Protection/Suppression research focuses on understanding the mechanisms of initiation, flame spread, combustion, mitigation, and suppression of combat initiated fires, with particular emphasis on petroleum, oils, and lubricants. Research includes mechanistic modeling, platform flame models, and novel experimentation. Additionally, improved concepts for flame protection are conceived and researched.

Counter CBRNE Threats research includes understanding emerging technologies and maturing solutions that support counter Chemical, Biological, Radiation, Nuclear, and Explosives (CBRNE) research. The technical focus is centered on developing devices or methods to combat weapons of mass destruction and eliminating CBRNE hazards through the ability to detect, assess, characterize, advise, and mitigate CBRNE hazards.

SCIENCES FOR LETHALITY AND PROTECTION's Weapon-Target (Lethal) Interactions S&T Footprint	
S&T AREA	**POSTURE**
Penetrators & Warheads	LEAD
Munition Response	LEAD
Disruptive Energetics	LEAD
Armor	LEAD
Soldier Personal Protective Equipment	LEAD
Hit Avoidance Technologies	LEAD
Active, adaptive, and collaborativeprotection	COLLABORATE
Fuze, S&A, Sensors	COLLABORATE
Decoys and Obscurants	COLLABORATE

Fire Protection/Suppression	COLLABORATE
Counter CBRNE Threats	WATCH

ELECTRONIC WARFARE research concentrates on understanding, exploiting, and protecting against the effects of directed and non-directed application of energy across the electro-magnetic spectrum for the purposes imposing desired effects or preserving mission effectiveness.

Electronic Attack/Protect research is dedicated to exploring and conceiving of means and technologies to exploit electro-magnetic energy across the spectrum for effective fires and protection. Electronic attack and protect includes the use of electro-magnetic radiation to analyze, locate, target, illuminate, jam, spoof, disrupt, damage, and their appropriate protection countermeasures against electronics, sensors, electro-optic devices, structures and non-lethal technologies against personnel. Research in this area concentrates on solid-state devices which operate across the spectrum from the ultraviolet (UV) to radio frequencies (RF). Cyber technology is not included in this definition of EW.

Historically, the electronic attack approach was to use high power microwaves at close ranges to cause damage and upset effects of electronic targets of interest. While effective in early theater operations, this approach was not sufficiently adaptive to changes in operation tempo. Smart jamming techniques incorporating device forensics is our current approach to electronic attack. This requires an understanding of how to inject or couple RF energy onto a target for either a neutralize or alternative effect. We identify and define waveforms or modulation techniques and validate these effects in our RF chambers.

One challenge is digital RF memory (DRFM). DRFMs pose a threat to our radar assets because it provides an almost perfect return signature. An objective of this program is to identity artifacts from a DRFM signature and devise new radar waveforms that are hardened from the DRFM spoofing.

RF Directed Energy is focused on mechanisms and concepts for efficient anti-personnel and anti-materiel use of RF directed energy and protection from RF directed energy. Smart jamming and damage techniques incorporate device forensics where waveforms are indentified and defined. This requires an understanding of how to inject or couple RF energy onto a target to either neutralize or cause an alternative effect. Challenges include miniaturizing RF components, reliable phased arrays, and adequate power levels in SWaP packages.

Laser Directed Energy research is focused on mechanisms and concepts for the development of efficient solid state lasers operating in the UV (<250 – 395 nm), near Infrared (0.8-2 microns) and midwave Infrared (3-5 microns) spectral bandwidths. These lasers cover pulsewidths from continuous wave to ultrashort laser pulses at femtoseconds or less. Applications include jamming, spoofing and/or damage to infrared missile seekers, tracking and illuminating lasers and enabling technologies for high energy lasers the cause structural and/or sensor damage such as countering rockets, artillery shells, mortar rounds, and missiles (C-RAMM), counter UAS, and counter sensors. Challenges include, achieving adequate power levels in solid state lasers within SWaP contraints, adequate frequency and wavelength control, beam control, thermal management, beam combining, diode laser coupling, understanding beam propagation in all atmospheres.

Sensor and Eye Laser Protection focuses on understanding vulnerabilities and providing protection of sensors and eyes from laser threats so that there is no degradation of visual performance in the presence of a laser threat. Laser protection goes beyond fix line filters to address frequency agile protection, high energy laser protection, short pulse protection, structural protection. Challenges include reduction of optical cross section, broadband fast response over large field of view, thermal management and understanding material and device failure.

RF Protection focuses on understanding device vulnerabilities and employing efficient and effective methods of RF countermeasure technologies such as waveform generation and shielding technologies. Challenges include identifying artifacts from a digital RF memory (DRFM) signature and devise new radar waveforms that are hardened from DRFM spoofing.

SCIENCES FOR LETHALITY AND PROTECTION's Electronic Attack S&T Footprint	
S&T AREA	**POSTURE**
RF Directed Energy	COLLABORATE
Laser Directed Energy	COLLABORATE

SCIENCES FOR LETHALITY AND PROTECTION's Electronic Protect S&T Footprint	
S&T AREA	**POSTURE**
Sensor and eye protection	COLLABORATE
RF Protection	COLLABORATE

BATTLEFIELD INJURY MECHANISMS concentrates on understanding and exploiting the fundamental aspects of human combat injury mechanisms.

Human Response to Threats research is focused on gaining a fundamental understanding and insight into how mechanisms of injuries and degraded human behavior manifest themselves in the grounds forces threat environment. Research interests include understanding how the human brain is damaged in blast and impact events; and uncovering underlying physical damage mechanisms and linking them to biological mechanisms and neurological behavior.

Humans in Extreme Environments studies the response of various human life systems to extreme environments associated with military operations. Of particular interest is the ability to understand and probe and model the macro-mechanistic biological response to man-made threats in order to postulate and conceive potential practicable materiel solutions to mitigate threat impact, increase combat effectiveness, and mitigate injury severity thereby reducing degradation of short and long term life quality and/or cost of care.

Tissue behavior studies the fundamental mechanistic response of human systems and how they may be affected by lethal and non-lethal weapons interactions. Understanding these mechanisms will permit the postulation and conception of novel means, potentially cross-disciplinary, to mitigate or control the human response to various threat stimuli.

SCIENCES FOR LETHALITY AND PROTECTION's Human Response to Threats S&T Footprint	
S&T AREA	**POSTURE**
Humans in Extreme Environments	COLLABORATE
Tissue behavior	LEAD

Human Protective Equipment research is dedicated to understanding mechanisms of threat human interaction and establishing equipment to provide protection against non-primary threats (natural environmental conditions, noise) while non-inhibiting mission function or provided additional capability for protection against primary threats.

Vision/Hearing Protection research characterizes requirements of protective devices in terms of degree of Soldier protection, perceptual performance capability and interoperability with other Soldier protective equipment. ARL perceptual research is a leading resource for human factors design guidance for industry and RDECs tasked with development of Soldier eyewear, hearing protection, and communications systems

Environmental Protection Research aims to develop materials that protect against heat, cold, sun and other natural human stressors. It includes the development of fabrics and personal protective equipment that wick away moisture, retain heat, prevent overheating and at times simultaneously protect other non-natural threats. It also includes the development of Soldier injury models that account for stress and fatigue as a function of natural human stressors such as heat and IR signatures. Finally, it follows closely human factors research that ensures that no protective clothing interfere with Soldier performance or the function of other protective gear.

SCIENCES FOR LETHALITY AND PROTECTION's Mechanical Failure of Tissue S&T Footprint	
S&T AREA	**POSTURE**
Vision/hearing Protection	LEAD
Environmental Protection	COLLABORATE

HUMAN SCIENCES CAMPAIGN

MISSION: To discover, innovate, and transition S&T capabilities to (1) understand and improve individual and small unit performance across the full range of military operations; (2) empower leaders with enhanced cognitive capabilities to make sound decisions quickly; and (3) enable expeditionary forces to use knowledge of societal and cultural issues and social cognitive networks to shape the operational environment.

VISION: The Army of 2030 maximizes the effectiveness of Soldiers physically, perceptually, and cognitively. Small units are capable of operating effectively and efficiently in social-cultural contexts around the globe. The desired end state is to leverage the full range of S&T enablers to poise forces to succeed in distributed operations and increasingly complex environments.

HUMAN SCIENCES CAMPAIGN PLAN

ARL's Human Sciences Campaign is focused on identifying, creating, and transitioning scientific discoveries and technological innovations underlying Human Behavior, Human Capabilities Enhancement, and Human-System Integration that are critical to the U.S. Army's future technological superiority. This campaign concentrates on high-risk and high-payoff transformational basic research; critically-focused, promising applied research; and selective advanced technology development that are expected to have revolutionary impacts on the Army's warfighting capabilities. In addition to significantly improving the Army's existing warfighting capabilities, it creates disruptive and game-changing Soldier-centric technologies for the Army, while also preventing technological surprises from potential adversaries.

The Human Sciences Campaign provides a critical assimilation point for Soldier-relevant technologies across all of the other ARL Campaigns. Human Sciences incorporates technologies and concepts from the other plans into multi-scale, human-centric research and advanced technology development, while concurrently feeding deep knowledge of human function, states, behavior, and performance, as well as human-based and human-systems technology concepts, into the other campaigns. Human Sciences is executed with ARL's in-house scientists and engineers who collaborate directly with world-class extramural researchers and technology developers. When unique and important opportunities exist, research is also executed in collaboration with industry, academia, not-for profit organizations, and other U.S. and international researchers.

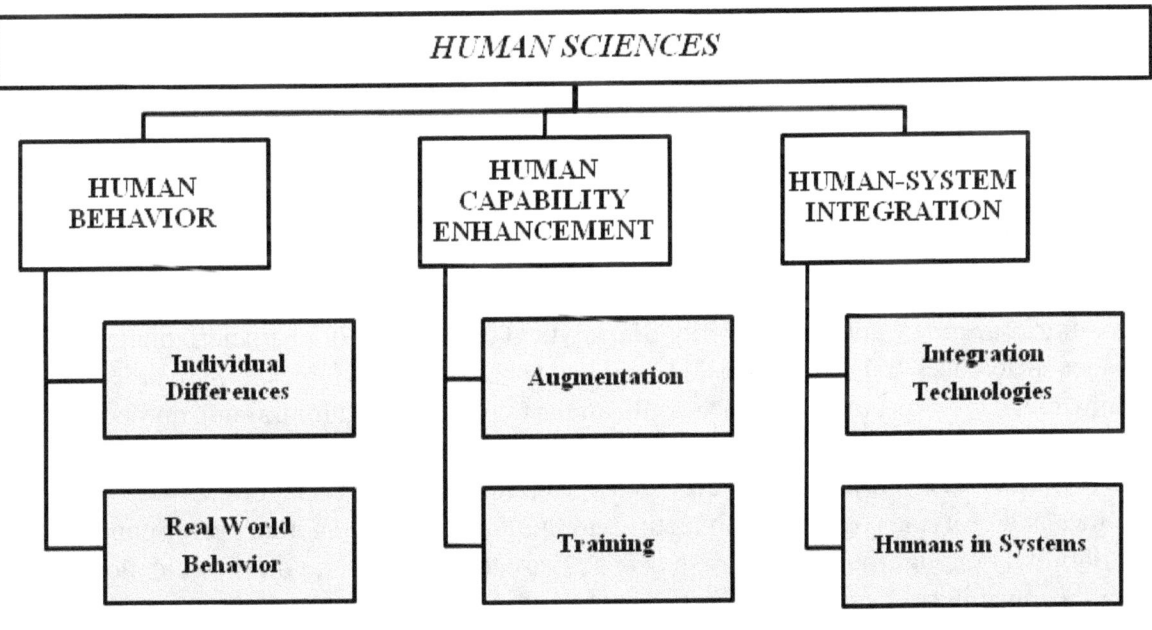

Levels 1 through 3 of the *HUMAN SCIENCES* Campaign Plan Taxonomy

HUMAN BEHAVIOR encompasses basic and applied research, which aims to discover, understand, and predict human perceptual, cognitive, affective, physical, and social behaviors in settings ranging from individuals and teams to organizations and societies. Human Behavior research focuses on critical research gaps necessary to transition extant knowledge and new discoveries into innovative technologies that are expected to create revolutionary capabilities for the Army of 2030 and beyond. Innovations in this area are expected to generate capabilities to predict warfighter performance and provide fundamental enablers for enhancing Soldier capabilities and maximizing Soldier-system performance well beyond the capabilities of today's Army.

Individual Differences supports research to discover and understand the underlying properties, principles, and mechanisms governing the differences between individual humans that are expected to lead to new methods, algorithms, and capabilities for predicting dynamic individual performance within a range of settings from small units to societies. Innovations are expected to enable revolutionary capabilities to individualize equipment and technology design, uncover mechanisms that underlie individual differences in resilience, and training for Soldier augmentation and systems integration for the purposes of enhancing mission performance and capitalize on diversity within the population.

Individual Behavior is focused on discovering and characterizing factors that influence variability in task performance between people across multiple timescales. This area includes novel experimental paradigms and modeling methodologies to understand the link between behavioral and physiological measures and fluctuations in performance across a variety of perceptual, cognitive, and physical tasks. Applications of this knowledge will enable the individualization of a broad breadth of technologies.

(i) Brain Networks focuses on capturing functional and structural brain connectivity using recent innovations in multimodal imaging techniques to capture neural fluctuations underlying behavioral performance at multiple timescales.

(ii) State-dependent Behavior employs high resolution behavioral and physiological responses to identify, characterize, and classify task-relevant states, such as stress and fatigue, that influence performance outcomes.

(iii) Emerging Scientific Innovations follows research and technology advancements in the study of biomarkers across scales in the human nervous system to map across multiple microstructure and macrostructure levels as well as computational cognitive psychological methods to quantify behaviors at multiple time scales. Numerous fields of research and technology are being watched including but not limited to molecular biology, biochemisty, genomics and genetics, terascale volumetric analysis, and rapid and high-resolution microscopy.

Models and Methods investigates advanced computational approaches that improve the resolution, accuracy and predictability of analytical techniques for characterizing performance differences and decision-making strategies between individuals. Discoveries and innovations are expected to produce applications to enhance Soldier training and performance.

(i) Cognitive and Neural Models leverages advances in computational processing capabilities and unifying cognitive architectures to build models that capture performance variability, ranging from variability in task strategy to differences in multi-scale models of brain connectivity.

(ii) Enhanced Quantification and Prediction investigates analysis methods to improve the detection, characterization, and classification of task performance and dynamic human states; to predict the influences of human states on an individual's behavior; and to predict task performance.

HUMAN SCIENCES CAMPAIGN's Individual Differences	
S&T Footprint	
S&T AREA	POSTURE
Brain Networks	WATCH

State-dependent Behavior	WATCH
Emerging Scientific Innovations	WATCH
Cognitive and Neural Modeling	COLLABORATE
Enhanced Quantification and Prediction	WATCH

Real World Behavior focuses on a multi-scale understanding of human behavior within real world contexts and environments to include fundamental discoveries of the properties and principles of mechanisms governing individual behavioral dynamics. Innovations focus on approaches and technologies to translate laboratory-based research findings to real world applications, as well as discovering novel technologies to interpret behavior under real world conditions. Discoveries and innovations are expected to yield capabilities that will dramatically improve Soldier training, in-field performance, and human's use of technology.

Human Performance is focused on multi-scaled understanding the effects of new technology on the performance of Soldier related tasks in the real world. This line of research advances previous efforts by developing an understanding of the underlying principals by which equipment affects performance in place of merely characterizing the effects of equipment on performance.

(i) Cognitive-Physical Interactions specifically studies the effects of new technology on physical and cognitive burden, and the resulting effects on the performance of Soldier related tasks in operational environments. This line of research seeks to develop new methods for collecting typical laboratory-based, high-resolution Soldier performance data in real world environments.

(ii) Small Arms Shooting Performance focuses primarily on understanding the effect of weapon design characteristics (recoil, new weapon technology and/or accoutrements) on shooting performance, and on developing methods and metrics for collecting shooting performance data in more operationally relevant environments.

(iii) Effects of Overburden on Small Team Performance studies the effects of individual performance on the performance of small teams. This emerging research area seeks to develop new ways of quantifying small team performance in operationally relevant environments, to better understand how Soldier burden (both physical and cognitive) is distributed through a small team, and how this distribution affects the performance of that team.

Realism in Simulation aims to develop a fundamental understanding of the Soldier's performance across immersive environments of varying fidelity. The knowledge gained will characterize the level of human-machine interaction necessary and the development of immersive simulation tools, methods and technologies that can effectively increase Soldier's performance across military tasks.

(i) Environmental Fidelity is focused on delineating the relationship between training environment immersiveness and Soldier performance and behavior to characterize the level of physical, perceptual, and cognitive interaction needed to be effective for the type of tasks to be performed.

(ii) Displays, Graphics, and Immersion consists of the development of new techniques for creating and displaying photorealistic computer graphics of people, objects, and environments, resulting in computer-generated virtual models of varying levels of realism.

(iii) Intelligent Character Behavior is focused on research to explore and evaluate techniques to rapidly create and re-use human characters with intelligent and adaptive behaviors across simulation and training systems.

(iv) Synthetic Natural Environments is focused on research to rapidly develop realistic synthetic geospatial databases that can be used across live, virtual and constructive simu-

lations and training applications. Research includes techniques to enable real-time, dynamic geospatial databases with physics-based effects. ARL leads this research area and collaborates with industry and the National Geospatial Intelligence Agency.

(v) Commercial Games and Interfaces advances are watched, to apply new techniques and technologies developed by the entertainment industry to improve realism of human character behavior in virtual simulations, new game engines with enhanced fidelity and new interfaces that allow for natural human-machine interactions.

Enhanced Interpretation focuses on approaches, methodologies, and technologies to improve the interpretation of human data within real world environments across multiple scales and dimensions. Discoveries and innovations are expected to yield capabilities that will dramatically improve Soldier capability enhancement and in-field performance.

(i) Real World Neuroimaging aims to enable the interpretation of measures of brain function as humans interact in real world environments as well as the interpretation of dynamic changes within individuals resulting from real world activities.

(ii) Pervasive Multi-Aspect Approaches follows research and technology advancements in the continuous monitoring of humans through multiple sensor and network approaches for durations from weeks to years.

HUMAN SCIENCES CAMPAIGN's Real World Behavior S&T Footprint	
S&T AREA	**POSTURE**
Cognitive-Physical Interactions	COLLABORATE
Small Arms Shooting Performance	COLLABORATE
Effects of Overburden on Small Team Performance	WATCH
Environmental Fidelity	LEAD
Displays, Graphics, and Immersion	COLLABORATE
Intelligent Character Behavior	COLLABORATE
Synthetic Natural Environments	COLLABORATE
Commercial Games and Interfaces	WATCH
Real World Neuroimaging	COLLABORATE
Pervasive Multi-Aspect Approaches	WATCH

HUMAN CAPABILITY ENHANCEMENT is a basic research, applied research, and advanced technology development effort, which aims to discover, innovate, and develop technologies that directly and indirectly enhance human perceptual, cognitive, physical, and social capabilities ranging from individuals and teams to organizations and societies for the Army of 2030 and beyond. Innovations in this area are expected to generate equipment and training technologies that will provide unprecedented capabilities for future warfighters and enable future leaders to make sound decisions effectively in complex socio-cultural contexts.

Augmentation focuses on research to understand and augment fundamental human capabilities across short and long time scales. Augmentation aims at enabling greater capabilities, providing resilience to durations of limited capabilities, and supporting agile, knowledgeable decision making. Innovations in augmented sensory and cognitive systems that are matched to individual capabilities and tuned to the operational environment are expected to significantly impact warfighter situational awareness and decision making. Innovations are also expected to enhance warfighter physical capabilities by balancing load, improving protection, and enhancing performance.

Perception aims to characterize and augment the perceptual requirements of visual, auditory, and tactile signals in complex, dynamic, militarily relevant environments. Models of perceptual detection, recognition, and spatial orientation are derived from laboratory and field studies and provide guidance principles for the materiel development community.

(i) Auditory research includes the study of recognition, identification, and spatial perception of military-relevant sounds and speech as a function of noise and personal protective equipment (PPE) use.

(ii) Visual research is used to develop models and training programs for improved natural target recognition and the design of night vision devices.

(iii) Multisensory research characterizes ways that multimodal cues provide redundant information at times and interfere with accurate situation awareness at others.

(iv) Vibrotactile psychophysical research aims to optimize the integration of a head-mounted tactile display with bone conduction as a dual-use system. The Human Sciences Campaign leads this novel application of technology.

Cognitive/Affective focuses on augmenting capabilities that include the mental and emotional skills necessary for Soldier performance in military relevant situations, including personal and situational awareness; interpretation, perception, reasoning, memory integration, and judgment; and consequent action such as reflective regulation and decision making. Discoveries and innovations are expected to yield applications of electrical, chemical, or biological stimulation to the nervous system, as well as technologies to assist in developing mentally resilient Soldiers, preventing injury, and re-bounding from injury.

(i) Cognitive/Affective Augmentations aims to provide and evaluate technologies designed to enhance cognitive and affective capabilities. Augmentations also address confounding factors to cognitive/affective resilience such as sleep, stress, and the ability to focus attention.

(ii) Cognitive/Affective Resilience aims to enhance the capacity of a strained individual, team, or unit to overcome significant adversity and recover its cognitive and affective capabilities following hardship and deformation.

(iii) Neurostimulation follows technology advancements in direct stimulation of neural tissue with electronic devices for incorporation into broader human systems. Several specific technologies are being watched including transcranial direct current stimulation, transcranial magnetic stimulation, and deep brain stimulation.

Physical focuses on 'skin-out' technology that may augment physical performance, and focuses on advanced technology designed to increase the physical strength of the Soldier or increase their endurance. As described below, exoskeletons and physical resilience technologies differ relative to the types of task they are designed to augment. This research area does not investigate pharmaceuticals or other technologies that may fundamentally affect the Soldier's physiological processes.

(i) Exoskeleton research follows the class of Soldier-borne technology and control algorithms that can increase the physical strength or power of a Soldier through mechanical augmentation. This technology can be active (powered) or passive (unpowered). This research area seeks to understand and measure the effects of exoskeletons on the performance of Soldier relevant physical tasks in both laboratory and operational environments. Additionally, research results are transitioned to exoskeleton designers to influence design for usability and comfort.

(ii) Physical Resilience follows research, technology advancements, and advancement in control system algorithms aimed at increasing endurance and mitigating deleterious effects of physical load and duration of event (prolonged load carriage) on Soldier

physical performance and state. Several areas of research are being watched, including devices designed to reduce metabolic cost and to speed the recovery from the performance of prolonged Soldier physical tasks.

HUMAN SCIENCES CAMPAIGN's Augmentation S&T Footprint	
S&T AREA	POSTURE
Auditory	LEAD
Visual	COLLABORATE
Multisensory	COLLABORATE
Vibrotactile	LEAD
Cognitive/Affective Augmentations	WATCH
Cognitive/Affective Resilience	WATCH
Neurostimulation	WATCH
Exoskeleton	COLLABORATE
Physical Resilience	COLLABORATE

Training includes a broad-based program of fundamental research and advanced technology development to achieve significant advances in Soldier training and, ultimately, mission effectiveness. The development of future training technologies requires advances in learning sciences, human sciences, human-system interaction, computer science, engineering and modeling and simulation. Execution of the training technology program is intended to produce high-payoff achievements in learning, retention, and transfer of knowledge and skills from the training environment to the operational environment. The end goal is to discover and innovate powerful new tools, technologies, and methods that can accelerate learning, can be applied at the point of need at any time and are affordable.

Effectiveness and Learning Methods includes fundamental research and advanced technology development of training effectiveness tools and learning methods to enable effective, efficient and adaptive/tailored instruction to enhance learning. Potential applications include adaptive tutors that dynamically adapt instruction to the Soldier's state, automated training effectiveness tools, and distributed learning environments.
(i) Adaptive Tutoring focuses on the investigation of methods to enable Computer-Based Tutoring Systems (CBTS) to adapt instruction, based on learner states (cognitive, affective, and competence) with the goal of optimizing learner outcomes consisting of performance, retention, accelerated learning, and adaptability.
(ii) Training Effectiveness focuses in determining the degree to which a system facilitates training on targeted objectives. ARL leads the Army's efforts to determine the needed technologies for efficient, reliable and valid training effectiveness evaluations.
(iii) Distributed Learning aims to investigate and evaluate a technology-enabled, data-driven, learning environment for integrated, distributed training across multiple platforms (personal computers and mobile devices) consistent with the Army Learning Model.
(iv) Artificial Intelligence (AI) Methods advances are watched to learn about new AI methods in numerous sub-areas such as Machine Learning (systems that can learn from data) and Data Mining (computational process of discovering patterns in large data sets by different methods).

Simulation and Training Technology investigates, demonstrates and advances a broad range of simulation technologies to enhance Army training. Potential applications include augmented reality training environments, virtual humans, live training and simulation technology, medical simulations and embedded training.

(i) Virtual/Mixed and Augmented Reality aims to innovate training environments, models, and human-machine interaction capabilities to support realistic training in virtual, mixed and augmented reality simulations.

(ii) Virtual Humans is focused on the development of techniques to rapidly create computer-generated characters with human-like behavior that can be used as role players in Army simulation and training systems.

(iii) Live simulation technology investigates and develops technologies to significantly enhance the realism of live training events across Military Operations on Urban Terrain (MOUT) sites, ranges, home station and Combat Training Centers. This includes but is not limited to the development of a new generation laser system for the Multiple Integrated Laser Engagement System (MILES) program.

(iv) Medical Simulation research consists of prototyping the most realistic and effective simulation-based training systems for Soldiers and caregivers by advancing the state-of-the-art in key enabling technologies consisting of silicon and synthetic biological tissues; odors; blood and other body fluids; variable physiology; sensors; after action review capabilities; 3D anatomy; and virtual patient visualization.

(v) Embedded Training consists of research into the integration of models and simulations into Army ground and air platforms to conduct training and mission rehearsals. Specifically, ARL is evaluating and maturing enemy prediction software for integration with Army mission command systems.

(vi) Advances in Computer/Network IT for training simulation and technologies is an Army area of interest in the academic and industry sectors consisting of new computing technologies, data distribution capabilities, cloud technologies, internet advances, mobile devices, and social media and processes with training and combat operational applications.

HUMAN SCIENCES CAMPAIGN's Training S&T Footprint	
S&T AREA	POSTURE
Adaptive Tutoring	COLLABORATE
Training Effectiveness	COLLABORATE
Distributed Learning	COLLABORATE
Artificial Intelligence Methods	WATCH
Virtual/Mixed and Augmented Reality	COLLABORATE
Virtual Humans	COLLABORATE
Live	COLLABORATE
Medical	COLLABORATE
Embedded Training	COLLABORATE
Advances in Computer/ Network IT	WATCH

HUMAN-SYSTEM INTEGRATION includes basic and applied research that aims to discover, understand, exploit, and apply fundamental principles of human-system integration across domains, including but not limited to complex information systems, human-agent teams, cybersecurity, and organizational and social networks. Discoveries of fundamental principles governing *networked communications and human-system relationships and dynamics are expected to lead to* technological and methodological innovations critical in poising the Army of 2030 to quickly shape its operational environment. These discoveries are expected to be relevant across the full range of social and cultural environments.

Aspects of this research complement efforts in the Computational Sciences Campaign, the Information Sciences Campaign, and the Extramural Basic Research Campaign, with the delineation being that research in the Human Sciences Campaign places greater emphasis on the influences of the human-in-the-loop system on the dynamics of human behavioral performance and effectiveness; approaches for stable, agile, adaptive control based on individual human capabilities and states; and human influences on overall system design and effectiveness. Additionally, the Human Sciences Campaign leverages work in the Assessment and Analysis Campaign on Human-System Integration tools and methods development.

Integration Technologies research is focused on innovations in core areas underlying human-system integration. This effort seeks to discover, understand, and exploit the properties, principles, and mechanisms governing human-system interactions to innovate novel interfaces and stable, robust, effective control systems, as well as developing approaches to analyze, model, and predict effective human-system integration. Innovations are expected to enable human integration in varying-sized sociotechnical systems that are more effective, naturalistic, tightly coupled, and more adaptable to the dynamic user than found in today's Army.

Interface Technologies examines cutting-edge applications and concepts in human-system interface design, including the cognitive and behavioral impact of information display modalities and system control interactions. Novel approaches and techniques for enhancing the accuracy, effectiveness, and throughput of information between user and system are sought. Innovations are expected to enhance information-based human-system interactions that increase Soldier-system performance and unburden the Soldier by decreasing cognitive and training demands.

(i) Multi-modal Interfaces focuses on interfaces that combine multiple modes of outputs and inputs to improve the accuracy, effectiveness, and throughput of information between user(s) and system.

(ii) Intuitive and Naturalistic Interfaces examines the cognitive and behavioral impact of information display modalities and system controls on human users and seeks to develop interface design principles that unburden the Soldier by decreasing cognitive demands and dramatically reducing training.

(iii) Implantable Materials/Devices follows technology advancements that are leading to the emerging field of implantable interfaces. Examples of areas being watched include sensors, computers, and controls implanted in teeth, under the skin, taken orally or directly interfaced with neural tissue.

Closed-Loop Behavior focuses on the conceptual, computational, and biological bases of the intrinsic dynamic behaviors that are unique to closed-loop human systems. Emerging approaches to adapting and enhancing closed-loop human-system behavior are also considered. Applications are expected to exploit the dynamic nature of closed-loop human-system behavior to improve the integration of human and system in innovative Soldier technology solutions.

(i) Cybernetics seeks to identify general systems principles that operate across levels of analysis and incorporate these principles within new methodological and analytical approaches that capture the temporal dependencies inherent to human data, emphasizing descriptive, mechanistic, and predictive models of human behavior.

(ii) Brain-Computer Integration aims to discover novel approaches to interpreting information from brain signals and seeks to uncover fundamental principles and innovative approaches to adapting and enhancing human-system behavior based on direct inputs from neural signals.

HUMAN SCIENCES CAMPAIGN's Integration Technologies S&T Footprint	
S&T AREA	**POSTURE**
Multi-modal Interfaces	COLLABORATE
Intuitive and Naturalistic Interfaces	COLLABORATE
Implantable Materials/Devices	WATCH
Cybernetics	COLLABORATE
Brain-Computer Integration	COLLABORATE

Humans in Systems focuses on discovering, understanding, and exploiting fundamental principles governing the influences of the human-in-the-loop system on human dynamics and effectiveness. This effort also focuses on the human influences on overall system design and effectiveness on human-agent teams, cybersecurity, and organizational and social networks. Innovations are expected to exploit a fundamental understanding of aspects of social network dynamics; organizational structure optimization; and ethics, values, trust, social-cultural, economic, and geopolitical effects. This will enable the development of advanced technologies that influence group dynamics and performance.

Human-Agent Teams investigates issues related to human collaboration with agent systems in small-team settings. This effort focuses on human trust in agents, agent transparency, cognitive robotics, and human-agent teaming. Research efforts seek to understand the interaction processes for the human and agent team members, reliably measure human-agent trust and teaming, and develop agent capabilities based on cognitive architectures. These topic areas apply to human interaction with virtual agents, physical robots, and heterogeneous agent teams.

(i) Trust examines interactions between the human and agent partners that have impacts on humans' calibration of trust in the agent systems. Specifically, this effort focuses on agent self-explanations and transparency (agent conveying information of reasoning, uncertainty, and projection of future outcomes) and trust measurement development.

(ii) Cognitive Robotics seeks to enhance, augment and refine existing Artificial Intelligence algorithms using cognitive architectures and psychological theory. This effort focuses on landmark-based navigation, episodic learning, and object recognition. Potential research areas include context recognition, situation understanding, and conceptual formation.

(iii) Human-Agent Teaming examines the processes of human collaboration with agent systems. This effort focuses on human interaction with intelligent agents for robot management, human-agent shared mental models, and metrics for human-agent teaming. Application areas include physical robots, virtual agents, and heterogeneous agent teams.

(iv) Dynamic and Individualized Interactions follows research efforts on human interaction with multiple distributed agents with emergent behaviors. Efforts on advanced information visualizations in other domains are also closely followed.

Socio-Technical Systems is focused on socio-technical network operations and human cognition, with the goal of improving distributed collaboration and decision making in complex operational environments. The payoff is improved Soldier decision-making, communication as well as unit performance and capabilities in complex network-enabled operations. Both socio-technical properties and Soldier cognition are considered in order to align Soldier and system capabilities.

(i) Data-to-Decisions aims to apply principles from the cognitive, computer, and social network sciences to the "data to decision" requirements of complex dynamic network-en-

abled operations. Conduct research using models and methods to support distributed information processing and decision-making spanning tactical to strategic networks, focusing on enabling Soldiers to manage and exploit information in complex and dynamic environments.

(ii) Decision Support Systems consider Soldier intent, state of the world, and domain specific knowledge to recommend a course of action. Soldier and unit performance is improved by shortening the cycle time from data gathering to decisions. The program approach uses a doctrinally-based knowledge representation to model role-specific workflows and continuously monitors the state of the operational environment to enable decision-support, delivering the right information to the right person at the right time.

(iii) Human Dynamics of Cybersecurity. The overarching scientific goal of this effort is to develop a rigorous science of cyber-decision making enabling military environments to: (a) detect the risks and cyber-attacks present in an environment, (b) understand and predict the motivations and actions of users, defenders, and attackers, (c) alter the networked environment to securely achieve maximal operation success rates at the lowest resource cost.

(iv) Networked Team Performance aims to leverage and build upon communication technology to quantify human dynamics in complex teams. The Human Sciences Campaign collaborates to advance the Army's ability to unobtrusively monitor Soldier and team performance over time to enable proactive support and human augmentation.

(v) Intelligent Systems and Social Dynamics focuses on human-system teams in social environments, where social cues and context will impact performance. Important components include understanding the social cues used in human communication, how social and cultural context influence performance, and development of design principles to instill social/cultural understanding in human-systems interaction.

(vi) Socio-Cultural Influences focuses on developing a validated socio-culturally informed Soldier/Commander decision-making taxonomy that influence asymmetric threat's decision and planning cycles as input to models and information tools. Representative algorithm models of social cultural variables will be developed and integrated into ARL's Culturally Aware Asymmetric Threat (CAAT) model along with methods and metrics to assess and improve Asymmetric threat forecasting.

(vii) Ethics and Values watches research and technology advancements to consider development of ethical systems to impact human-system performance, particularly relevant in interactions with intelligent, adaptive, and reasoning systems.

HUMAN SCIENCES CAMPAIGN's Humans in Systems S&T Footprint	
S&T AREA	**POSTURE**
Trust	COLLABORATE
Cognitive Robotics	COLLABORATE
Human-Agent Teaming	COLLABORATE
Dynamic Individualized Interactions	WATCH
Data-to-Decisions	COLLABORATE
Decision Support Systems	COLLABORATE
Human Dynamics of Cybersecurity	COLLABORATE
Networked Team Performance	COLLABORATE
Intelligent Systems and Social Dynamics	COLLABORATE
Socio-Cultural Influences	COLLABORATE
Ethics and Values	WATCH

ASSESSMENT AND ANALYSIS CAMPAIGN

MISSION: To discover, innovate, and transition S&T capabilities that (1) improve the technologies being developed to meet critical and Army-unique needs; (2) provide decision makers and Soldiers with accurate and detailed awareness of materiel's capabilities; and (3) link the institutional and operational forces by means of a powerful shared toolset that simplifies and improves their decision making.

VISION: Army decisions about technology investments, weapon systems acquisition, and operational employment are founded on rigorous, transparent technical bases that take account of the full DOTMLPF spectrum, the breadth of adversaries' potential actions and countermeasures, and the ultimate consequences in terms of our forces' effectiveness in completing their missions. The desired end state is that comparable analytical capabilities are built into materiel and fielded to operational units, allowing Soldiers to employ swiftly and decisively emerging Army systems.

ASSESSMENT AND ANALYSIS CAMPAIGN PLAN

ARL's investments in Assessment and Analysis have three aims – supporting evaluators, Program Managers (PMs), and decision makers; modernizing Army's capabilities for the laboratory's historic strengths in engineering-level analyses of technologies and systems; and leveraging those strengths to create fundamentally new capabilities. Accomplishing these aims will position ARL to lead the Army to the RDT&E solutions that will be demanded by technological and strategic realities, the evolution of which will only continue to accelerate.

ARL's Assessment and Analysis Campaign is focused on guiding the development and integration of technologies, substantially broadening the range of issues that can be addressed with analytical rigor, improving the throughput and responsiveness of the analytical processes, and developing ruggedized and ready-to-employ applications that make the full power of the laboratory's internal analysis capabilities available directly to the Army's operational force. This campaign builds on fundamental pillars of physics, materials science, mechanical engineering, mathematics, and chemistry to conduct analyses in areas including *Ballistic Susceptibility; Electronic Warfare; and Materiel Failure.*

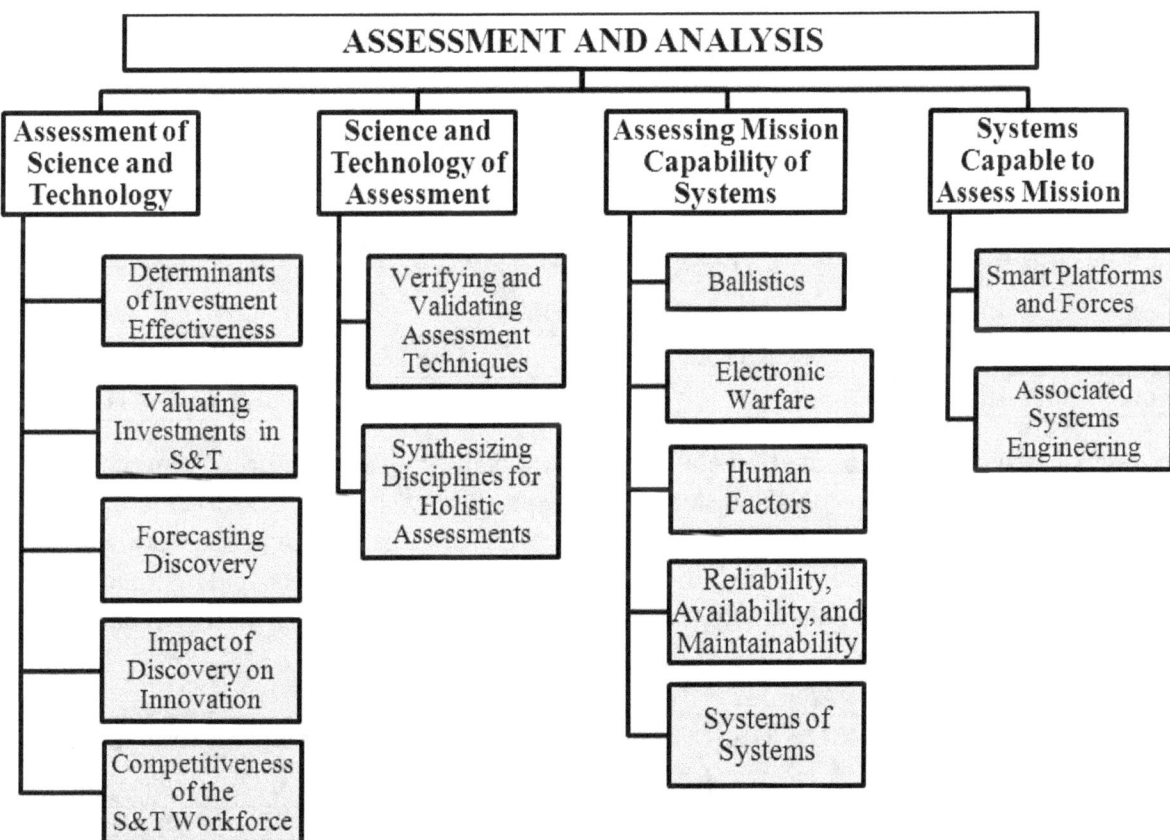

Levels 1 through 3 of the Assessment and Analysis Campaign Plan Taxonomy

ASSESSMENT OF SCIENCE AND TECHNOLOGY concentrates on understanding the costs and benefits of R&D efforts, their readiness levels, risks, potential payoffs, and integration challenges.

Determinants of Investment Effectiveness concentrates on identifying and maturing quantitative models or decision analysis tools that show promise as effective mechanisms for evaluating investment efficiency of research and development (R&D) programs. Methodologies developed through these efforts are expected to provide an alternative approach to "expert-review panels" to ascertain R&D program investment effectiveness.

ASSESSMENT AND ANALYSIS CAMPAIGN'S Determinants of Investment Effectiveness S&T Footprint	
S&T AREA	**POSTURE**
Investment Effectiveness Assessment	COLLABORATE

Valuating Investments in S&T concentrates on identifying and maturing quantitative models or decision analysis tools that show promise in estimating the impact of budgetary investments on S&T productivity – over the near-term as well as over an extended time period. Methodologies matured through these efforts are expected to provide insight into valuation trend trajectories with sufficient lead time to enable active management engagement.

ASSESSMENT AND ANALYSIS CAMPAIGN'S Determinants of Investment Effectiveness S&T Footprint	
S&T AREA	**POSTURE**
Investment Valuation	COLLABORATE

Forecasting Discovery concentrates on identifying and maturing quantitative models or decision analysis tools that show promise as effective mechanisms for using assessment of recent S&T advances to forecast new discoveries or new areas of discovery. Methodologies developed through these efforts are expected to provide an alternative approach to "expert-review panels" to discern promising areas for new scientific discovery.

ASSESSMENT AND ANALYSIS CAMPAIGN'S Forecasting Discovery S&T Footprint	
S&T AREA	**POSTURE**
Discovery Forecasting	COLLABORATE

Impact of Discovery on Innovation concentrates on identifying and maturing quantitative models or decision analysis tools that show promise as effective mechanisms to determine the scientific discoveries that are expected to lead to the highest-impact innovations; levels of understanding that are required to launch the most fruitful innovation efforts; and approaches to reconcile long-term innovations leading to promising recent discoveries within the context of customer-driven requirements.

ASSESSMENT AND ANALYSIS CAMPAIGN'S Impact of Discovery on Innovation S&T Footprint	
S&T AREA	**POSTURE**
Impact of Discovery on Innovation	COLLABORATE

Impact of S&T on Innovation and Competitiveness concentrates on identifying and maturing quantitative models or decision analysis tools that show promise as effective mechanisms to assess the impact of the scientific enterprise on U. S. technological innovation and corporate competitiveness world-wide. These efforts are expected to lead to assessment approaches that enable identification and rigorous assessment of scientific enterprise-wide attributes which influence technical innovation trends and corporate market share dynamics – both critical to realizing technology-enabled capabilities for the future Army.

ASSESSMENT AND ANALYSIS CAMPAIGN'S Impact of S&T on Innovation and Competitiveness S&T Footprint	
S&T AREA	**POSTURE**
Scientific Enterprise Assessment	COLLABORATE

Competitiveness of the S&T Workforce concentrates on identifying and maturing quantitative models or decision analysis tools that show promise as effective network analysis mechanisms to assess the scientific labor force formation. In particular, these efforts are expected to be critical in ascertaining the quality of the STEM workforce; barriers of entry into the scientific workforce for post-secondary STEM graduates; types of technical organizations that attract post-secondary STEM graduates; and developing technical labor market trends.

ASSESSMENT AND ANALYSIS CAMPAIGN'S Competitiveness of the S&T Workforce S&T Footprint	
S&T AREA	**POSTURE**
S&T Workforce Assessment	COLLABORATE

SCIENCE AND TECHNOLOGY OF ASSESSMENT concentrates on understanding the key types of analytical problems likely to confront the Army of 2030, exploiting the latest developments by our academic and industrial partners, and performing basic and applied research to develop the powerful new tools required.

Verifying and Validating Assessment Techniques is focused on improving our ability to provide stakeholders and customers with assessments that are technically compliant, accurate, precise, usable, and defensible. Robust verification and validation is critical to managing the risk of flawed decisions resulting from assessments that are inadequate or erroneous. The goal of these efforts is to pursue mathematical and statistical methodologies to enable reliable verification and validation of a broad array of phenomena and systems.

ASSESSMENT AND ANALYSIS CAMPAIGN'S Verifying and Validating Assessment Techniques S&T Footprint	
S&T AREA	**POSTURE**
Verification and Validation Assessment	COLLABORATE

Synthesizing Disciplines for Holistic Assessments is focused on developing rigorous, general methods to establish metrics and algorithms for combining distinct, heterogeneous phenomena without sacrificing either fidelity or incurring unacceptable artifactual error. These efforts are expected to lead to rigorous methodologies to treat multiple phenomena within a single, coherent context.

ASSESSMENT AND ANALYSIS CAMPAIGN'S Synthesizing Disciplines for Holistic Assessments S&T Footprint	
S&T AREA	**POSTURE**
Robust Algorithm Development	COLLABORATE

ASSESSING MISSION CAPABILITY OF SYSTEMS concentrates on understanding and exploiting systems' technologies, design, and employment together with current – and likely future – state of the art developments to optimize future designs and to inform evaluation and acquisition decisions with analyses that are both technically sound and practically efficient. Key to this effort, are methodologies to integrate technical assessments into the science and engineering domain with considerations of mission effectiveness for the materiel's operational user.

Ballistics is focused on analysis of the effects of blast and ballistic loading on the brain and the body, and will incorporate numerical models of Soldiers into system level analyses of performance predictions. This research is expected to enable system performance prediction to analyze the costs and benefits of changes in any portion of the system up to overall Soldier performance. Complementing this research is an extensive program of physical and virtual experiments to develop the empirical data necessary to validate these tools. This work augments work conducted in the Human Sciences Campaign.

ASSESSMENT AND ANALYSIS CAMPAIGN'S Ballistics S&T Footprint	
S&T AREA	**POSTURE**
Ballistics Analysis	LEAD

Cyber focuses on assessing the vulnerability of Army acquisition systems – networks and devices connected to the network – to cyber threats. Assessment and Analysis cyber analysts conduct red teaming, blue team vulnerability assessments (VA), penetration testing, and code analysis utilizing existing methodologies, tools and techniques and developing those needed to assess new technologies. This augments and leverages work being conducted in the Information Sciences Campaign.

Device is focused on performing VA of devices, particularly the analysis of the software code; and penetration testing. The Assessment and Analysis Campaign's efforts in this area consist of developing software VA tools to automate penetrations testing and code analysis. The campaign leverages off-the-shelf tools, products, and techniques from other government agencies, academia, and industry.

Network is dedicated to conducting VA of the Army's networks against cyber threats to support acquisition decision milestones is a new technical problem. The Assessment and Analysis Campaign works with the T&E community to define metrics and develop methodologies to evaluate the performance of these networks. The campaign applies best practices and subject matter expertise in support of the independent evaluator; and leverages and utilizes technological breakthroughs that result from research performed in the Information Sciences Campaign.

ASSESSMENT AND ANALYSIS CAMPAIGN'S Cyber S&T Footprint	
S&T AREA	**POSTURE**
Device Assessment	COLLABORATE
Network Assessment	COLLABORATE

Electronic Warfare is focused on development of new methodologies and techniques to assess the impacts of emerging Electronic Warfare threats. Areas of particular interest include the impacts of dynamic Electronic Attack threats on communications systems and ultrashort-pulsed lasers on optical sensors.

Communications is focused pursuing development of a new generation of electronic countermeasure techniques, waveforms, models, simulations, and methodologies to conduct theoretical, laboratory, and field investigations to counter dynamic Electronic Attack (EA) threats – with an emphasis on vulnerability analyses to support the Army's Test and

Evaluation community. In particular, Radio-frequency (RF) communications systems revolutionized by dynamic spectrum access (DSA) developments; multiple-input, multiple-output (MIMO) antenna systems; and ultrawideband signaling techniques are of interest.

Sensor Vulnerability is focused on better understanding ultrashort-pulsed laser threats and their impacts on the Army's optical sensors. These efforts concentrate on understanding emerging laser threats that are likely to occur in the battlespace, development of novel assessment methodologies, and improving existing models. These efforts are integrated with work in the Materials Research Campaign.

ASSESSMENT AND ANALYSIS CAMPAIGN'S Electronic Warfare S&T Footprint	
S&T AREA	POSTURE
Communication System Analysis	LEAD
Sensor Vulnerability	LEAD

Human Factors is focused on pursuing and developing integrated Human Factors Engineering (HFE) and System Engineering (SE) assessments and analytic techniques to produce effective models capable of predicting human, system, and mission capabilities early in the acquisition cycle. These efforts concentrate on identifying human capabilities and limitations within the physical, perceptual and cognitive areas, and will be leveraged by the Human Sciences Campaign.

Physical is focused on incorporating the understanding gained in the Human Sciences Campaign into analysis, assessment tools, and techniques to generate novel modeling and simulation (M&S) methodologies envisioned to be capable of evaluating the physical capabilities and limitations of the human and the system. M&S techniques produced through this effort are expected to enhance Army's capacity to make predictions of systems' mission capability and provide inputs to efforts dedicated to Human Factors.

Perceptual is focused on incorporating understanding of human perception and design principles, leveraged from the Human Sciences Campaign, into analytic modeling & simulation (M&S) tools and techniques to provide quantitative, enhanced predictions of human perceptual performance. Modeling & Simulation (M&S) tools and techniques developed as a result of these efforts are expected to provide Analysts with enhanced prediction capabilities to produce human and system for effective mission capabilities that prevent Soldier overload that would otherwise lead to increased injury, fratricide, and contribute to decreased system and mission performance.

Cognitive is focused on incorporating understanding of human cognition – including translational neuroscience directed at exploring the relationship between the brain's physical structure, its dynamic neurophysiologic functioning, and human behavior – leveraged from the Human Sciences Campaign, into analytic modeling & simulation (M&S) tools and techniques for early, cost effective insertion of HFE & SE criteria requirements within the acquisition process that are designed to optimize Soldier-system performance, mission capability and cost.

ASSESSMENT AND ANALYSIS CAMPAIGN'S Human Factors S&T Footprint	
S&T AREA	**POSTURE**
Physical Modeling and Simulation Techniques	LEAD
Perceptual Modeling and Simulation Techniques	LEAD
Cognitive Modeling and Simulation Techniques	LEAD

Reliability, Availability, and Maintainability (RAM) is focused on pursuing and developing new methodologies and techniques to facilitate assessments of personnel and materiel readiness.

Personnel is focused on developing a human-availability metric to express human downtime as a function of inherent system reliability, supportability concept, and human-to-task functional allocation. Inputs to the metric will be system failures caused by operator error; downtime resulting from performing critical system tasks – start-ups, reboots, shut-downs; and downtime due to awaiting field service representatives and their maintenance actions.

Materiel is focused on developing methodologies to assess the impact of Reliability, Availability, and Maintainability (RAM) on the mission capability of systems. This effort will couple real-time sensing of the environment and system status – microscopic through macroscopic scales – with physics-based modeling of the mission-based demands on the system to determine margin to failure. This capability is expected to aid technology developers in optimizing designs; planners in optimizing mission load; and operators in optimizing courses of action on the fly to allow the mission to be accomplished.

ASSESSMENT AND ANALYSIS CAMPAIGN'S Reliability, Availability, and Maintainability (RAM) S&T Footprint	
S&T AREA	**POSTURE**
Personnel	COLLABORATE
Materiel	COLLABORATE

Systems of Systems (SoS) is focused on developing new analysis capabilities for a system of systems (SoS) – a collection of interlinked and mutually dependent systems that has properties and capabilities well beyond the simple union of the independent attributes of its constituent systems. Novel analysis capabilities developed as a result of these efforts are expected to provide accurate representations of battlefield effects such as ballistic events, computer-network operations, and electronic warfare, embedded within cognitive, communication, and decision-making contexts.

ASSESSMENT AND ANALYSIS CAMPAIGN'S Systems of Systems (SoS) S&T Footprint	
S&T AREA	**POSTURE**
Technology	COLLABORATE
System	COLLABORATE
Systems Engineering	COLLABORATE

SYSTEMS CAPABLE TO ASSESS MISSION concentrates on understanding and exploiting developments in the other S&T campaigns to evolve assessment and analysis itself from a laboratory service to a technology that we transition to the warfighter.

Smart Platforms and Forces is focused on developing analytical models and simulations which can be used to augment or replace assessments traditionally done by a highly skilled workforce.

Human Decision Making is focused on integrating knowledge from ARL's Cybernetics research program into analytic models and simulations to represent the synergy of an optimum human-machine interface. In these representations, feedback from the humans to the system will indicate when the human is overloaded, and the humans' tasks will be dynamically allocated to the system. As a consequence of the task reallocation, the human operators of the system will have evenly distributed manageable workload and, thus, will be better able to make effective decisions.

Aware and Adaptive Training is dedicated to developing next-generation learning-management systems (LMS) that dynamically track and evaluate each Soldier in the systems that they operate. The LMS is expected to be integral in determining performance gaps, recognizing training needs, and then delivering appropriate training automatically to greatly increase the units' operational readiness and direct towards their particular missions. In addition, the LMS would enable leaders to continually assess their Soldiers' training readiness.

ASSESSMENT AND ANALYSIS CAMPAIGN'S Smart Platforms and Forces S&T Footprint	
S&T AREA	**POSTURE**
Human Decision Making	COLLABORATE
Aware and Adaptive Training	COLLABORATE
Systems Engineering	COLLABORATE

Associated Systems Engineering is focused on identifying and mitigating the unintended consequences and potential vulnerabilities that systems engineered smart capabilities may introduce into the battlespace. In particular, these efforts are dedicated to developing systems engineering concepts specifically envisioned to holistically accommodate smart technologies, systems, platforms, and forces while minimizing or wholly eliminating interoperability and fundamental functionality challenges.

ASSESSMENT AND ANALYSIS CAMPAIGN'S Associated Systems Engineering S&T Footprint	
S&T AREA	**POSTURE**
Holistic Systems Engineering for Smart Platforms and Forces	COLLABORATE

www.ingramcontent.com/pod-product-compliance
Lightning Source LLC
Chambersburg PA
CBHW080256290526
45790CB00005B/1826